Adva

With great skill and compassion, Joan E. Childs has written a thoughtful and insightful exploration of intimate relationships, complete with the struggles, conflicts, and disappointments, which few of us can escape. She presents steps we can all take to build resilience and intimacy. Her message is clear, inspiring, and instructive. I encourage women everywhere to abandon their guilt and grab a hold of this book! If you've ever thought of leaving the man you love—the same one who can drive you to orgasm *and* anger in the same day—this book is essential reading.

—Susan G. Furman, psychologist, psychoanalyst, and couples therapist

Leave it to Joan E. Childs to come up with a book title that could make most heterosexual women say "Yes!" She displays a passionate attention to detail that matches her extensive training in the field, along with her keen interest and expertise in working with couples. She combines that with charm and a witty sense of humor, making her latest book, *I Hate The Man I Love*, an entertaining, compelling, and ultimately helpful read.

—Eileen J. Cohen, LMFT, MCAP

A refreshingly important read! *I Hate the Man I Love* is written from the unique vantage point of a seasoned psychotherapist who not only specializes in couple's therapy but has first-hand experience as a multi-divorced single parent with five children. In relating the stories of several female clients, Childs examines—with real candour and wit—the conflicts and resolutions of each participant while offering professional wisdom.

—Nancy Rosenfeld, Literary Agent, AAA Books Unlimited

In *I Hate the Man I Love*, a unisex and omnisexual journey to benefit us all, Joan E. Childs summarizes the many lessons and daily obstacles that derail couples, families and individuals. Gleaned from her long personal and professional challenges, the book is academic and practical and will touch every reader who will recognize and find aid for familiar situations.

—Avram M. Cooperman, MD, FACS

With sensitivity and skill, Joan E. Childs gets right to the heart of the stumbling blocks all couples inevitably encounter in long-term relationships. The title of the book says it all. Sometimes we really *do* hate the man we love! Through fascinating case studies and exercises, Childs provides the tools we need to repair and renew our union.

—Christine Belleris, senior editor, Health Communications, Inc.

Joan E. Childs is a generous friend, a trusted colleague and an admired mentor. With more than 40 years of experience in the field of psychology and relationship therapy, she's showing no signs of slowing down! She continues to bless us with her wisdom and experience. In her latest book, *I Hate the Man I Love,* Joan has captured the essence of what it means to be female and our struggles to understand complex love and our attachment to men. Through theoretical and case studies, Joan leads us on a fascinating journey that is both pragmatic and mystical. She's a great writer and this is a book worth reading and saving on your bookshelf.

—Mary Kay Cocharo, LMFT
Certified Imago Relationship Therapist
Practitioner of Encounter-centered Couples Therapy

I Hate the Man I Love is an enthralling journey that explains how childhood trauma can lead us to "hire and fire" our spouses (life partners) as we work through our issues. Childs uses vibrant, raw stories to depict the levels of commitment we are capable of giving to our partners, along with coping tools we can use to "clean the environment" and create a sacred, safe space. This book has explained the conflicts in my relationships and given me tools to avoid communication gaps in the future. Thank you, Joan, for making the second half of my life easier to navigate!

—Anne Melby, RMT, PMP, Senior Operations Executive

As a vintage professional with vast personal experience, Joan E. Childs examines the microscopy of interpersonal angst with full-blown, highly palpable clinical vignettes, which pique our interest from the outset. Her title captures the crucial theme and central tasks of most relationships. As a board-certified psychiatrist, with a practice similar to Joan's, this book reflects what often happens behind the closed doors of a psychotherapist's office. Her powerful examples of dysfunctional relationships and the various methodologies she uses to break down barriers to true intimacy, demonstrate how she enables the development of healthy, durable relationships. The book also reviews renowned therapists and philosophers, adding texture and depth to a well-written work.

—Jack Baruch, MD
Diplomate of the American Board of Psychiatry and Neurology

I Hate the Man I Love captures the true nature of the challenges we face in contemporary relationships. Joan's foundational knowledge of the best theorists and practitioners in the field are a perfect complement to her 40-plus years of professional experience. The technique exemplified in Chapter 7 is spot on for healing the wounds of our love relationships in a culture full of communication/connection chasms. Whether you're in a struggling relationship and longing for more love and connection, or a clinician fine-tuning your expertise, this book is both invaluable and essential. Read away and watch the relationship transformation manifest!

—Lisa Kelly Cargerman, PhD. MFT, Boulder, Colorado

Written in an engaging, understandable style, *I Hate the Man I Love* allows the reader to be a fly on the wall at couples therapy as they uncover relationship conflicts, which often result from unconscious childhood traumas. Licensed clinical social worker, Joan E. Childs, shares her personal and clinical experiences to offer evidence-based approaches for those struggling in relationships, as well as for therapists working with clients addressing these issues. Equally skilled as a captivating presenter and an eloquent author, Joan's book is filled with the same wisdom and charisma she displays as a professional trainer, which she has done for MHASEFL's Continuing Education (CEU) programs. Satisfying relationships are a core element for maintaining good health, and this book provides the necessary strategies to achieve that goal.

—Marcia Pinck, Director, Florida Counseling Services
Education & Outreach, Mental Health America of Southeast Florida

If you are looking for an informative, comprehensive and practical book about the essentials of a conscious relationship, look no further. In *I Hate the Man I Love*, Joan E. Childs delves deep into the soul of our human connections. She eloquently illuminates the complex and layered paradoxes of love, as well as the multi-generational secrets of Re-Pair, restoring our pair-ship. Weaving together psychological insight, science, practical examples, and storytelling, Joan richly gifts us with "New Eyes" to successfully navigate our relationship journeys towards Relational Maturity.

—Hedy Schleifer, Master Relationship Builder, Founder, EcCT (Encounter-centered Couples Transformation)

Joan Childs is that rare and super-natal writer whose own deep emotional insight illuminates the pages of her book with personal examination of human connection—sometimes in strong productive relationships. Sometimes at the depths of despair from broken ties, alienation, or the pain of affairs that have failed, been broken or have disintegrated.

—Richard Cravatts, PhD, President Emeritus of Scholars for Peace in the Middle East, Author, *Dispatches From the Campus War Against Israel & Jews* and *Genocidal Liberalism: The University's Jihad Against Israel & Jews*

As Childs peels back the complex layers of relationships, she provides running commentary as she also portrays both partners through empathic eyes, inviting vulnerability and newfound respect for mutual discovery. You will see yourself in her pages. Read this riveting book!

—Myles K. Krieger, MD, Life Coach Board of Directors, American Friends of the Hebrew University

I Hate the Man I Love

A Conscious Relationship Is Your Key to Success

I Hate the Man I Love
A Conscious Relationship Is Your Key to Success

Joan E. Childs, LCSW

Frederick Fell Publishers, Inc.
1403 Shoreline Way
Hollywood, Florida 33019
www.fellpub.com
email: fellpub@aol.com

Frederick Fell Publishers, Inc.
1403 Shoreline Way
Hollywood, Florida 33019

I Hate the Man I Love
First Edition.

Published in the United States of America by Frederick Fell Publishers, Inc.

10 9 8 7 6 5 4 3 2 1

Library of Congress Cataloging-in-Publication Data

Childs, Joan E.
I hate the man I love : a conscious relationship is your key to success
    / Joan E. Childs, LCSW.
    p.cm.
Includes index.
LCCN 2020002219 (print) | LCCN 2020002220 (ebook)
ISBN: 978-0-88391-489-2 (pbk.: alk. paper)
1. Couples–Psychology. 2. Man-woman relationships–Psychological aspects.
    3. Interpersonal relations. 4. Interpersonal conflict. I. Title.
HQ801 .C4788 2020   HQ801
306.7–dc23

For information about special discounts for bulk purchases, please contact Frederick Fell Special Sales at fellpub@aol.com or call 945-455-4243.

ISBN : 978-0-88391-489-2
eBook : 978-0-88391-490-8

To Judith,
and all the women
and couples I have
counseled.

Contents

Foreword

I tell my students that when my husband Yumi and I married in 1965, we were the Olympic champions of unconsciousness. Neither of us had any idea that there was such a thing as a conscious relationship.

Ernest Hemingway says: "The world breaks everyone and afterwards many are strong at the broken places."

Yumi and I began to explore how to become connected to each other from the "broken places" in our relationship. Expanding on what T.S. Eliot says about seeing a familiar place with new eyes, we arrived at a surprising discovery: our relationship is not a problem to be solved. It is an adventure to be lived and a gift to be unpacked. We discovered a guiding principle and three invisible connectors with which to productively live this adventure.

This is the guiding principle: what will always disconnect us is the inevitable, reactive power struggle of our survival dance as a couple; what will always connect us is the mutual embrace of the three invisible connectors. The survival dance is our automatic reactivity to perceived danger in the relationship, which we import from our childhood narrative.

The three invisible connectors are: the Space, the Bridge, and the Encounter.

As a couple we are responsible for the quality of the relational space. It is a sacred space and the playground of the children we bring to the world. We honor that relational space by crossing the Bridge to the world of our partner, to discover their culture and language. In doing so we become bi-lingual, and create together the conditions to experience the magic of what Martin Buber calls the Encounter—a heart-to-heart and soul-to-soul connection.

I was fortunate to meet Joan Childs 13 years ago, at an important juncture in my own life. I had been married to Yumi for 41 years and had just decided to create a Master Class for experienced Couples Therapists. I wanted to explore and share the Relational Paradigm and the Encounter-centered Couples Transformation method, which had evolved from the living laboratory of my own marriage. To my delight, Joan, a seasoned psychotherapist, and a person of experience and integrity, became an active participant in my Master Class, a three-year deep dive into the Encounter-centered Couples Transformation method.

In *I Hate the Man I Love* Joan integrates her more than 40 years of experience as a psychotherapist with "new eyes" for the Relational Paradigm. She says in the Introduction that, "Conflict is part of all relationships. It is not something to run away from because it becomes a friend, especially when a couple uses it to cleanse their relational space that too often becomes polluted over time.... When that space is cleansed, it becomes sacred and conscious, and the couple (and their children) feel safe again."

We live in a time where more and more we need to know how to genuinely be close to one another. My friend Lionel says of the smartphone: "It's a device that decreases the distance between people who are far away, and increases the distance between people who are close by." With our phones as indispensable as they have become in our daily lives, there is an urgent need for books about how to create conscious relationships.

This is the gift Joan offers. As you read, you will learn the skills to embrace and live the relational adventure. It is my greatest hope that you will come to enjoy the results that blossom in the living laboratory of your own relationships.

—Hedy Schleifer,
Master Relationship Builder

Introduction

The title of this book was born out of the mouths of some of my female clients—women caught up in a desperately messy mix of love and hate in their most important relationships. You might be one, too, someone feeling simultaneously hopeful and hopeless. If that's the case, keep reading.

This book is for you.

In more than 40 years of private practice as a clinical social worker, specializing in couple's therapy, and as a multi-divorced single parent with five children, I have learned many things, but one fact is crystal clear: more than 90 percent of my clients enter therapy due to a failing relationship, and nearly all of my sessions are initiated by the woman involved who is seeking help.

This is not to say that men don't ever make the first call, but it's rare. Men usually reach out only *after* their wives or girlfriends have threatened to end the relationship or have been served with divorce papers. At that point, it's often too late to repair what's been broken.

Women tend to reach out when they feel frustrated and disillusioned, hoping that a therapist like me can restore their relationship. They are hopeful that with the right counselor and a cooperative partner, things might get better by resolving conflicts and healing their relationship.

By making the first move—acknowledging a problem and seeking help—they are on their way to finding a solution to this strange phenomena of hating the man they love.

Let's be clear, though, that this is not a male-bashing book. In all fairness, men experience similar issues, albeit less frequently, and when they do they are not exactly willing to seek help. That's why this book might be the secret sauce they need. It might help some men become more aware and mindful that differences and conflicts with their partners can be negotiated when people decide to commit.

Aha! The 'C' word. Commitment is at the root of many issues we see couples face today. When it's lacking for any reason it illuminates the difficulties and frustrations women experience in their relationships with men, which is exemplified by the conflict we see repeating itself all the time: how oppositional feelings can simultaneously co-exist.

We can love our mate, but also feel at the same time that their behavior is intolerable. Sound familiar? Therapists refer to this condition as a love/hate relationship.

In Tony Bennett's song, Why Do People Fall in Love? he croons, "What is this feeling that hurts so good inside?" I'm sure you all know the feeling! This conundrum applies to how men and women feel about their partners, how parents sometimes feel about their children, and how children often regard their parents. It even affects us at work and in our communities.

As you read through the client stories in each chapter, revealing conflicts and resolutions, you will learn about rituals, principles and exercises. In addition to anecdotal and empirical data, I also present peer-reviewed evidence cited by professionals and researchers, all of whom have explored male–female relationships in great detail.

Their mission, and mine, is to understand the dynamics between the sexes and why more than 50 percent of marriages in the United States fail (with subsequent marriages having an even higher percentage of failure). I have studied and examined why emotional differences in men and women frequently result in ineffective or damaging communication, polluting the intimate and trusting space any relationship needs, which ultimately leads to crisis.

French novelist, critic and essayist, Marcel Proust said that, "The real voyage of discovery consists not in seeking new landscapes, but in having new eyes."

Throughout the book, I highlight universal issues and values that emerge in every relationship, including health (physical and mental), politics, money, race, religion, sex, gender, and culture. They are all part of the human experience, and the process of dealing with our differences is what matters. Only when we do, can we communicate and heal.

Women will find aspects in each chapter showing how differently they experience conflict in their relationships, such as how they report and complain about them in individual and couple sessions. These challenges are ubiquitous, pervasive and universal. Frustrations, which are applicable to gay and lesbian couples, as well, include issues such as not being present, stonewalling, judging, ignoring, poor listening and blaming.

We also include vignettes about women who are attracted to powerful men—celebrities, political figures, professional athletes, distinguished artists and wealthy businessmen and CEOs. These women pay a high price for their choices when they lose themselves in the effort to conquer their unconquerable guys. We see examples of this all the time, but these power struggles do not only exist on reality shows on TV. They are rampant on all economic levels, where an unhealthy perversion of power by one party over another can poison a relationship.

One story, about a woman held captive by her father in order to become his sex slave illustrates the power of the patriarch, which we cover in great detail in Chapter 2. Unfortunately, this story and many others included in the book, are all too relevant in how they portray women's contemporary experiences. Just turn on CNN, Saturday Night Live or one of many cable and network shows to see reports of how unhealthy relationships are causing huge problems, both at home and throughout the world.

Just as I always aim to help couples solve conflicts and repair and restore their relationship, this book provides valuable resources to help you maintain a healthy and harmonious union. They include the valuable work of several marriage and family therapists, such as John Bradshaw, founding father of the self-help movement, who hosted numerous PBS programs focusing on codependency, and spirituality, John Gottman, psychological researcher and clinician whose four decades of work on divorce prediction and marital stability led to The Gottman Method for developing lasting relationships, Esther Perel, a Belgian psychotherapist who promotes the concept of erotic intelligence in her book, *Mating in Captivity: Unlocking Erotic Intelligence*, Harville Hendrix, author of relationship self-help books, who, along with his wife, Helen LaKelly Hunt, is the creator of Imago Relationship Therapy, Lori and Morris Gordon, creators of the PAIRS program, and, most recently, the work of Hedy Schleifer, a renowned marriage and family therapist who provides workshops all over the world.

The contributions of these highly-respected experts has always informed my work and inspired the rituals and principles of a conscious relationship I am sharing here. While not every relationship can be healed and while some *should* end in divorce or breakup, it's essential to remember that each partner must be totally committed to the reparation of a relationship in order to achieve a substantial and meaningful result. Just as a marriage is best when both parties are fully committed, so can a divorce be done best when both parties try their best to do it well.

None of us is monolithic. We are created with different parts, like a rainbow consists of different colors. The total sum of our parts determine who we are and how we behave with others. What you will learn in the book is how to negotiate these parts so that they can live harmoniously.

This is what I do in my practice. Most folks are unaware of all their various parts, some of which are contradictory, and they struggle with internal conflict. This is normal. Consider the human body as a universe comprised of planets, stars, galaxies and other forms of matter and energy. Just as the universe represents the total sum of its parts, we humans follow a similar pattern.

That means don't be alarmed! It's perfectly normal for oppositional feelings to co-exist. It's common in parents with their children and vice versa, employees with their employers, and in a plethora of family and communal relationships. Very little is black and white.

We are all are perfectly imperfect. Just when you think you can't survive another minute with your man, your boss, your child, your mother-in-law, or your neighbor—let alone the rest of humanity— take a breath and calm down! This too shall pass.

I've been a therapist for four decades, which has taught me so much about human nature. Everyone is flawed to some degree. The challenge we all face is how we deal with this reality, i.e., our own flaws and those of our partner. What can you accept and at what price? Your task is to be honest with yourself and your partner, which I admit is easier said than done.

This book offers you a chance to investigate your relationships, to define genuine love in your life and make your relationship work. It's a bit like reading a book on swimming. The basic lesson is, you've got to jump in the water before you can learn to swim.

That's the idea—jump right in. It's your turn.

I imagine the title of this book initially caught your attention because something about it resonates for you or someone you care about. That's the point: to help you heal and restore your relationships. I use the plural of that word for a reason. Of course our primary focus is on the two people who constitute a marriage, but we all know that love/hate relationships can happen at home, at work, and within our community.

Acquiring the basic skills for managing these dynamics will play a valuable role that will yield positive results beyond your primary relationship. This book uses many clinical encounters from my practice to introduce and analyze issues and conflicts. Whenever possible, solutions are offered to help you avoid and resolve conflict while learning how to remain connected.

Conflict is a part of all relationships. It's not something to run away from because it can become your friend, especially when a couple uses it to cleanse their relational space that too often becomes polluted over time. When that shared space at home remains contaminated, it becomes hazardous, as each partner unwittingly reacts to a perceived or real danger occupying that shared space, affecting their life as a couple and a family. When that space is cleansed, it becomes sacred and conscious and the couple (and their children) feel safe once again. In fact, as each party begins to relax, an actual change can occur in the brain and the central nervous system.

When this happens, the couple can move their relationship forward. This is the thesis of the book—an adventure in intimacy with descriptive rituals and principles that heal the contaminated space.

In the words of Hedy Schleifer, whose TED talk, "The Power of Connection," has won rave reviews, "It is not a problem to be solved. It is an adventure to be embraced—a gift to be unpacked—a mystery to be understood and a secret to be uncovered."

Enjoy!

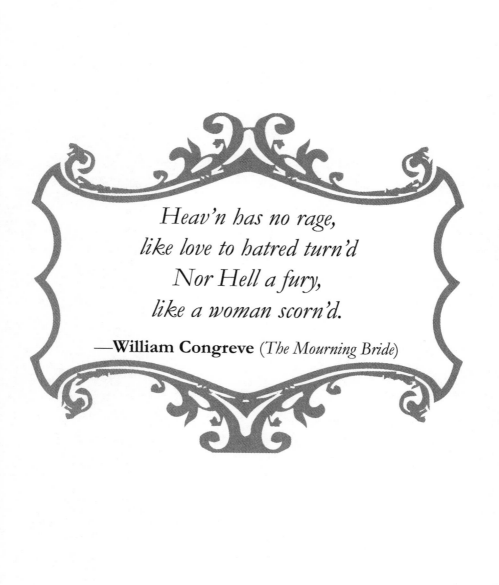

Heav'n has no rage,
like love to hatred turn'd
Nor Hell a fury,
like a woman scorn'd.

—**William Congreve** (*The Mourning Bride*)

1

Owning Your Choices

Whenever I welcome a new couple into my office for marriage counseling, I expect a few tense moments. After all, if everything was fine at home they wouldn't be here. But when Jackie walked in with her husband a few years ago, I was not ready for the fireworks she brought.

"I hate that man!" she said. "I hate him! I hate him! I hate him! He's an asshole, a worthless piece of shit! He's a son-of-a bitch, mother-f–ing, selfish bastard and I hate him!"

Before I could get a word in, she rose to her feet, flinging her Louis Vuitton bag over her shoulder, extending her neck stiffly while raising her chin to the ceiling in abject disgust.

"I'm done! &%$#@!"

Without waiting for my reaction or her husband's, Jackie stormed out of my office and slammed the door behind her. We could hear her continuing to curse out loud, as the sound of her high heels reverberated in the hallway on her way to the elevator.

I forced a smile for Allan, who sat in silence, blushing with embarrassment. He shrugged his shoulders, threw up his hands and apologized on behalf of his wife, seemingly clueless as to why she exploded in the first place. I had to wonder if this was accurate or if his blank canvas of a face was simply masking a much deeper problem.

How Did We Get Here?

Jackie was not the first woman who ever fled my office, her knuckles white with blind rage as she grabbed her handbag. Although not every woman carries a Louis Vuitton into my office, many of them do bluster off in a state of despair, carrying the burden of a troubled and even anguished relationship. Jackie was not the first and she won't be the last. However, on that day, when she exploded with such frustrated venom, the air in the room became so heavy so fast it felt like a blast of carbon monoxide had been blasted through my air conditioner. I felt an urgent need to walk out into the hallway to escape the toxins that Jackie had deposited on her way out. I excused myself for a few moments, as I had to take a few long breaths to restore my composure before I could return, sit calmly and face Jackie's apparently clueless husband.

As I took my seat in what is ordinarily a lovely comfortable chair, my mind was full of women's voices, in particular those deeply conflicted by their marriages. Before I could address Allen, who still appeared quite aloof and dumbfounded, I had to allow those voices their moment in my head before I could proceed.

"Sometimes I really hate him. I even despise him and wish I had never married him, but then there are times we have fun. We laugh together, enjoy a movie together, and just take a walk and hang out. But then as time goes on we share less time with each other and argue more. The tension becomes palpable and throws me into despair when the space between us feels polluted and unsafe."

"It will never get better. Sometimes I think I'd be better off without him."

"I want to feel like I did the day we said our vows. I want to feel excited when he takes me in his arms, but those days are gone. We go to bed with our computers instead of each other, and we wake up each morning to the same displeasure we had the night before. Will we live in quiet desperation for the rest of our lives?"

"What's going to happen when our kids leave and it's just the two of us? How lonely will that be? What will happen if I get sick and he's not present, or if he needs me in helpless moments in the years to come? Will my heart be in it, and will his be with me? What if I have a stroke or lose a breast, or if he develops Alzheimer's or prostate cancer? How can we have each other's backs if we live in two different worlds, like doomed ships passing in the night?"

"I want my husband back! How did we drift so far apart? I don't remember when he seemed to disappear. Maybe it was when I disappeared in his eyes, after the baby was born or when he got his promotion and started working longer hours."

"Does he even remember the color of my eyes? I ache to return to the days when he told me he loved me. I'm sure he does, but he doesn't express it anymore."

"When my husband gets annoyed he withdraws and I'm left alone feeling abandoned and dismissed. How can we restore our love and reconnect?"

Fess Up!

How often have you said these words under your breath, (or even in an outburst)? How many times have you had these thoughts, wanting to throw something at your partner or husband, muttering or spewing a declaration of war or divorce?

Be honest! Don't feel guilty—it's a common response that occurs with chronic frustration when you don't feel heard, validated, acknowledged, valued or respected—especially when nothing changes! Apologies are worthless when things stay the same.

You meet the love of your life, the man with whom you want to share your hopes and dreams. He's charming, warm, smart, handsome, sensitive and loving. He can't get enough of you and you of him. But then one day you turn a corner and out comes Mr. Hyde.

"Wait a minute! I didn't sign up for this. Where is Dr. Jekyll? Where is the man who swore to love and cherish me until death do us part? Who is this monster who came out of nowhere to torment me?"

Sound familiar?

He snores, he farts, he swears, and he never remembers to put down the toilet seat. The things you loved about him now piss you off. You don't remember this guy. He never listens, he talks over you, he lectures, and when you ask a question he replies with a one-word answer—his favorite being "Yes" or what's become even more familiar, the instinctive "No."

"Is this the same guy I wanted to grow old with?"

"Do other women have these issues and feel alone and unloved in their marriage or relationship? Or am I the only one who has lost herself and her partner during the course of all the time we've been together?"

You are not alone!

We're In This Together

These comments are typical of the diatribes I have continually heard from my female patients over all the years I have been in private clinical practice as a psychotherapist. Between the squeezed and painful tone of their complaints and the shrill sound of their anguished voices, echoing their desperate sentiments, I often couldn't help but want to cover my ears and run out of my office. Is that because any of them are so terrible? No, not at all. It's because I can relate all too well as a woman and a wife. The truth of the matter is that I have felt and said many of these things myself, more times than I care to admit.

It's no surprise under circumstances like these that we are left to wonder why we get into these messes in the first place and why we respond so poorly when they don't work out the way we thought they would or could or should. That's because our brains are hard-wired for making meaningful and trusting connections with people. When we experience a "disconnect" we go into crisis mode, as Jackie's reaction so clearly demonstrated. But of course she is not the only woman on such a situation.

For example, Ellen—just 30 years old and a brand new bride, had a meltdown less than 30 hours after her wedding. She and Mark had been living together for three years and Ellen had helped to subsidize the wedding and the townhouse they were living in, and she paid in advance for a honeymoon that never happened. She had been unable to receive any support from her new husband or family in assisting and cooperating with the wedding plans. Instead, she had been forced to go at it alone and she quickly became exhausted from trying to make it all happen by herself. Where was the groom or his or her family members? I never had a chance to find out. Ellen was trying to make something work that was never destined to succeed, and as soon as she realized that *after* the ceremony and the reception she became overwhelmed, anxious and exasperated with the lack of care or concern from her new husband. Her explosion in my office came as a result of her pent-up frustration and intense disappointment.

On top of that, Ellen suffered from depression, insomnia, anxiety and intractable pain since she had contracted Ankylosing Spondylitis and Fibromyalgia a few years earlier. These physical impairments, plus the emotional distress they created, had caused her to give up her job as an editor in a publishing company.

Once Ellen and Mark got home after the wedding, all hell broke loose. After she broke a vase expressing her rage, Mark, her brand-new, 30-hour husband, called the police and requested that she be Baker-Acted. This is a State of Florida mental health act, enacted in 1971, which allows for involuntary examination (what some also call emergency or involuntary commitment), which judges, law enforcement officials, physicians, or mental health professionals can initiate for a period up to 72 hours. There must be evidence that the person in question might possibly have a mental illness.

In an effort to stop Mark from calling the police and starting that process, Ellen charged at him, trying to get the phone out of his hands. In the ensuing struggle, she accidently knocked his glasses off, leaving him with a bloody laceration on his nose. This was the evidence he needed to prove that she was potentially harmful—to him and who knows who else—and which would qualify her for admission to the psychiatric ward of a local hospital.

Although she was evaluated on the same-day and discharged with no intention of harming anyone, including herself, Mark, the brand-new groom, decided right then and there that the short-lived marriage was over and the next day he went ahead and filed a petition for an annulment. He also locked Ellen out of their home, refused to return her belongings, and decided that she had been fraudulent with him by never revealing that she had issues with depression and anxiety, although according to her, he had known this since the beginning of their relationship, before they ever even moved in together.

What's Really Going On Here?

I have to jump in here and say that I find it hard to believe that Mark had no idea that Ellen was suffering from numerous ailments. No matter how hard she may have tried to conceal her struggles, how could he not have known *anything* about them? Can we take a chance and call him clueless or would that be presumptuous and a minor case of male-bashing? Since we don't want to be guilty of either charge, let's investigate further.

Under normal circumstances, Ellen would never have been considered a violent woman. With mitigating circumstances, however, surrounding the wedding, unable to properly attend to the details of her big day, coupled with dealing with intractable, chronic pain, with little or no support from her new husband, her inner beast rose up from the coals of hell, blowing dragon fire from the depths of her being. All the turmoil, frustration, and lack of communication became fodder for a perfect storm! There was no taming this shrew.

"Hell hath no fury like a woman's scorn!"

Shakespeare was right, to say the least, and I'm sure he would have winked at me if he had been a fly on the wall that day in my office. He was not the only one. Countless writers, psychologists, and philosophers have opined on how women in particular deal with the frustrations and angst they experience in their relationships. I have heard it from the source, over and over again, from women, myself included, who keep reminding me how different women are from men.

John Gray was absolutely spot-on when he wrote *Men Are from Mars, Women Are from Venus*, which has become the Bible for understanding the difference in our two genders since it was first published in 1992.

Meet Your Biology

Between all the therapy I have had and all the couples I have counseled, including Jackie and Alex and Ellen and Mark, Gray's words are endemic to living in any relationship between two sexes. I have continually asked myself over 40 years of practice why these words and feelings are so unrelenting. After all the creative marriage and couple-counseling techniques I have studied and practiced, and after all the various modalities I have subjected myself too, as well, how is that these sentiments continue to persist? I have finally figured out the answer. It requires understanding a bit of biology, coupled with acknowledging some crappy role-modeling and early interventions inscribed into the brains of boys who eventually become men.

"You wanna cry? I'll give you something to cry about!"

"What are you, a sissy? Boys don't cry! That's for sissies or girls!"

"Be a man! Act like a man!"

"You're not scared! Boys are strong. We're tough! Only girls get scared! Get over it!"

"You got feelings? I'll give you a feeling right in your face!"

These examples may sound a bit dated, especially if you consider yourself a "progressive" parent, but they can also take shape in more subtle ways.

"Come on, you're such a big boy. Big boys don't cry."

"Just throw me the ball. Throw it like a boy!"

"Act like a man? What are you, a girl?"

"Don't tell me you're scared like your sister, are you?"

"It's fine to have feelings, but boys shouldn't talk about them too much."

Back in the day, and still now in many cultures and sub-cultures, anytime a boy has a feeling, it is linked with shame or embarrassment, so boys consequently learn early in life not to feel, or at the very least, not to show them. If a situation became too emotional, everyone would vacate the premises, except perhaps for Mom and any other concerned women and/or girls. Any efforts by Mom to console her son were often interrupted with challenging comments, such as, "Don't baby him" or "Stop coddling him. He needs to toughen up!" As a result, boys grew up to become split off from any feelings of sadness or hurt. Anger became a more acceptable response.

"Somebody hit you? You hit them back!"

"Oh, Johnny hurt your feelings? Well then you go ahead and hurt his face!"

"Sticks and stones, boy, sticks and stones. Just shut up and play ball."

Anger is often a boy's first response to being hurt and this doesn't stop by itself when he becomes a man. Since boys are conditioned to feel shame for showing hurt or any sort of weakness, they use anger alternatively as a means of reacting, often to no good outcome. Girls, on the other hand, are often shamed if they get angry.

"Don't be sassy with me!"

"Girls are supposed to be little ladies, so act like one."

"Just sit there quietly until you get over yourself!"

Instead of showing anger, girls cry, almost like a default mechanism. That's why we end up with these results: Men get angry and women cry! If men could express their fear and sadness without feeling shamed, and women could express their anger without fear or shame, we would all live happily ever after! Sounds easy, but it's not.

Our Real Challenge

We now know that early imprints from society and parental attitudes at home form the foundation for our being. Neuro-biologists have substantiated and documented empirical evidence that our minds, personalities and behaviors are influenced more by our environment than our genes. It's true that genes give us a predisposition to who we become, but lifestyle, environmental factors and culture trump genes!

In *The Biology of Belief*, Bruce Lipton, PhD, an iconic cell biologist, draws evidence from studies in cellular biology that support his theory. The good news is that we *can* change, but only if we choose to and learn the appropriate ropes.

Hard to imagine? It's true. The results play out in our most important relationships—those we choose to be our life partners. This is not a blame game. If we had to blame our parents for poor parenting, we would have to go back to their parents, and the parents before them, and so on. That would quickly become futile and leave us taking no responsibility for who we are and how we behave. It also means we would shirk what should be a welcome responsibility as role models.

Our challenge and obligation in this one and only lifetime is to know what the hell happened to us and to take action so we can become conscious of our behaviors. Let me repeat:

We must be conscious of our own behavior and take responsibility for it!

Change is not only possible. It is necessary in order to enjoy a life of joy and fulfillment. As conscious beings, we can choose to make the changes necessary to live our lives in the sacred space we so longed for when we took the vows knowing absolutely nothing!

As young brides and grooms we know little or nothing about how our past influences our present. As adults and parents we are obliged to move our relationships forward and to make our relational space safe for each other and our children. This means learning about why we do the things we do and the effect it has on our life partner.

The Truth Always Surfaces

I have been fortunate to study psychology with the best of the best. I was trained in Practical Applications of Intimate Relationship Skills (PAIRS) with Lori and Morris Gordon, certified with John Bradshaw in Creating and Maintaining Healthy Relationships, attended workshops, seminars and lectures with Harville Hendrix, author of *Getting the Love You Want* and founder of Imago Relationship Therapy. I've studied the works of John Gottman, an American psychological researcher and clinician who has done extensive work on divorce prediction and marital stability, Sue Johnson, a psychologist specializing in bonding, attachment and adult romantic relationships, and who, along with Dr. Leslie Greenberg, developed Emotionally Focused Therapy (EFT) and founded the International Centre for Excellence in Emotionally Focused Therapy (ICEEFT), a therapist training institute. I have also researched Esther Perel, therapist, author, and creator of the groundbreaking podcast *Where Should We Begin*, and most recently, at the age of 75, I took a three-year Master Class called Encounter-Centered Couples Therapy, with a wonderful group of masters in their various therapeutic disciplines who brought great ideas, skills and methodologies to couple counseling, all led by Hedy Schleifer, whose TED talk, "The Power of Connection," describes the Three Invisible Connectors: the Relational Space, the Bridge and the Encounter.

In many cases, the results were miraculous, transformational and enduring. But eventually, after many two-day intensives and three-day workshops, the "I hate him!" energy would resurface and show its nasty ass once again. Couples who engaged in couple's therapy were at least aware of the cause, understood where it came from—even the implications and consequences—but were still not able to contain the feelings that were triggered in a split second.

When one partner felt triggered by a word, a look, silence, a judgment or dismissal, they acted out what came naturally, and that, we must all admit, is not always healthy. The shouting resumed, the tears and hysterics recycled, doors slammed, and the space that was once sacred became polluted and messy once again. Not surprisingly, the other partner usually became reactive or withdrew into what I call a silent violence, when the unconscious destructive dynamic rewinds and contaminates the sacred, relational space we must have to secure a healthy dynamic.

What Do We Do Now?

When each person in a relationship falls into their own survival mode, as if it's a default mechanism, the tension will always mount. It's a simple guarantee of biology and psychology, mixed together in a volatile combination. A person's essence gets lost in the muck and mire of conflict and they operate out of survival patterns they unwittingly learned in childhood.

In her workshop, An Adventure in Intimacy, Hedy Schleifer explains that couples unconsciously choose the perfect person to bring them the biggest nightmare to help resolve early childhood traumas. They unwittingly hire their partners only to fire them for doing the exact job they had hired them to do. What a conundrum!

This is an issue that has plagued men and women throughout the ages. It has been studied, researched and written about by scientists, biologists, social psychologists, psychologists, psychiatrists, neuro-biologists, philosophers, mental health providers, marriage and family counselors, sex therapists, social workers, clergy and even lay people.

Notice how I've referred both men and women being affected by these endless cycles. This is not about male-bashing or laying blame anywhere, other than with all of us. That's because we are all responsible for our choices, good, bad or somewhere in between. I intend to acknowledge, explain and provide answers to several age-old issues.

Let's move on with the mystery of biology and social conditioning, which continues to stimulate all women to figure out why men behave the way they do instead of acting more like us.

*"A bird may love a fish,
but where would
they build a home together?"*

—**Tevye**, from *Fiddler on the Roof*,
by Joseph Stein

2
Why Can't A Man Be More Like A Woman?

In the legendary Broadway musical, *My Fair Lady*, Henry Higgins, lamenting the current state of affairs between men and women—appears to ask a rhetorical question:

"Why can't a woman be more like a man?"

I prefer to take the opposite approach:

Why can't a man be more like a woman?

Although song and dance is not my specialty, if I could chant this phrase with the same inquisitiveness, wonder and curiosity that Rex Harrison possessed in his role as Henry Higgins I would definitely do so, without the clever British accent.

But what good is the question without an answer, so let's begin again.

"Why can't a woman be more like a man?"

Because she doesn't want to be! Period.

Why can't a man be more like a woman?

Essentially—because they're not!

We know all of this from biology, anthropology and social conditioning, and on paper it appears so damn simple, so why all the emotional fuss and perpetual problems?

When Henry Higgins appears to be tortured by the whimsical Eliza, it's simply because she is a woman who just wants to be herself. He becomes obsessed with making her into what he thinks she ought to be and desperately wants her to live up to his standards and expectations of femininity. As suspected, Eliza subjugates her will to his and becomes the elegant, fashionable Miss Doolittle he created as his fantasy woman.

The Stigma of Role Playing

I must emphasize the word fantasy, as this is largely what it was back then and still is. While Higgins takes the role of a Svengali in elevating Eliza from an impoverished flower peddler to become the belle of the ball it reeks of superficiality and seems quite unsatisfying in today's evolved climate. As much as Rex Harrison made Henry Higgins seem rather charming, what price did Eliza Doolittle actually pay? I mean, what happened to the authentic Eliza?

In an effort to please Henry Higgins, she loses her essence along the way. When she realizes she has been used for his own aspirations, she becomes enraged and enjoys a genuine fit of violence. She heaves his slippers and lunges at him, beating him with a vengeance so unlike the Miss Doolittle he once created. Her rage is finally unleashed and he has no clue as to why.

Hmm, sound familiar?

We might be relieved that it was just a play (and movie) and we can accept literary license to tell a story, but at what cost? What roles did this story perpetuate? In truth, Eliza was not so different than Jackie, the woman who stormed out of my office in a fit of rage while her husband looked on in dismay. Both of them were victims of society placing a stigma on their choice to be independent women, regardless of an unsupportive environment.

Repeating the Past

In the Broadway musical and movie, *Les Misérables*, a song called Master of the House fits the description of how so many women feel about their man. Unlike Tammy Wynette's Stand by Your Man, this resonates with most of the battered women I treat.

"Master of the house? He isn't worth my spit!"

"Comforter, philosopher and lifelong shit!"

"Cunning little brain, a regular Voltaire."

"Thinks he's quite a lover, but there's not much there."

"What a cruel trick of nature landed me with such a louse."

"God knows how I've lasted living with this bastard in the house!"

These lines are quite catchy and lend themselves to clever rhymes, but what about when some version of them are said by a woman who is not on a Broadway stage or in a film or on a concert stage? What about when one of these reactions is instigated by real life?

How many woman do you know who are living out the fantasy of what their male partners expect and demand?

How many of them are living a life of pain and torture for not feeling accepted as they are?

How many women are living their lives in either quiet desperation or have become shrews in a marriage that emulates what happens in Edward Albee's play, *Who's Afraid of Virginia Woolf?*

How many women, like Elizabeth Taylor first portrayed when she co-starred with Richard Burton, are currently surviving and perhaps even enjoying a sado-masochistic relationship?

These questions have been relevant for generations and despite whatever progress the women's movement has made, they are sadly still all too apparent in today's world. Many women continue putting up with behaviors from their mates that any psychotherapist would call abusive, tormenting, disparaging, insulting, disrespectful, inconsiderate and unacceptable.

Is it out of fear of never finding someone better?

Is it because of abject economic insecurity?

Is it that women stay put to protect their children from the risk of separation?

Perhaps the submission and capitulation we still often see is due to the supposed theory that the grass is never greener on the other side. Perhaps it originates with what these women know from having grown up in their families of origin.

Whatever the reason or rationale might be, women are guilty many times over of losing their essence for the sake of having a man.

A Deal with the Devil

The scary part is that many of them are not even aware of the tradeoffs they have made, such as security in exchange for authenticity, compliance in exchange for legitimacy, not rocking the boat in exchange for peace, and losing their voice in exchange for their essence. Are any or all of these just a recapitulation of their past? Are women who do these things reverting to choices that were once so familiar that it now feels normal or natural?

Either way, and for whatever reason, they are making a deal with the devil.

Sigmund Freud called this type of behavior *repetition compulsion*, which he described as the need to repeat the past. Alice Miller, psychiatrist and author of *The Drama of the Gifted Child*, called it "the art of absurdity," even though it has the identical meaning.

We only know what we know! Our brains are wired to perpetuate what is familiar. The past creeps into the present without warning or conscious awareness. All of a sudden, almost out of the blue, we find ourselves married to our father or mother, depending on which parent caused the most conflict and damage in their unwitting behavior or who we most identified with as a child.

In our effort to run from the past, we drag it with us into the present, finding a replacement for the person we are running from. In essence, we are addicted to our past and the only way we can break away from it is to understand the cause, but not just intellectually. It has to be relived in an experiential therapeutic setting with a trained professional. Instead, people opt for drugs as their preferred treatment, which usually only mask the symptoms instead of dealing with them in an effective way. Drugs, whether prescribed or illegal, are not the ultimate panacea. When dealing with the devil, genuine resolution takes process, time, money and commitment, which may be too much work for the average person. Divorce, which usually costs even more money, is often chosen as an optimum solution.

"We just weren't a good match."

"I've had enough."

"It was inevitable."

These are just a sample of what is often a typical explanation.

The Love/Hate Conundrum

How can I hate the man I love? Anyone reading this already knows the answer. It doesn't take an expert to know that "the dude" is not monolithic. He has a variety of parts, like we all do. He can be loving, generous, considerate, sweet, understanding, supportive and smart. He can also be intimidating, judgmental, unemotional, contemptuous, stonewalling and critical.

The most difficult behavior for a man is to be present and communicative as he at least tries to see your world through your eyes and ears, recognizing that you are carrying your past just as he is carrying his. Each of you are depositing your pasts into the relational space that is called "the relationship." After years of dysfunctional behavior, that space can become polluted and neither of you know how to fix it. When that happens, which is all too often, love flies out the window as the language of disillusion and frustration wields its nasty head. That's when the "I hate him" refrain reverberates through the windows of your mind and sometimes even your mouth!

What follows any of these reactions is some level of remorse for lowering your standard of acceptable behavior. The guilt and shame that come forth after harsh words are spoken is worse than the feelings that caused the initial clash.

The damage may already be done, however, because the words can never be retrieved. Only an apology can be offered with hope for forgiveness. In cases like this, all is well until it's not. As day follows night and night follows day, the pattern continues to return. It may reappear with different content but with the same results. The pollution mounts, the space is no longer safe, and the mutterings and spewing begin all over again.

This polluted space also becomes a toxic playground for your children and pets. Innocent animals know how to escape and hide under a bed. Children, not so much. Even worse, many children—of *all* ages—somehow feel responsible for the cause of their parent's strife and guilty for not being able to fix it. These feelings of helplessness become the foundation of their survival self. As they grow into adulthood, they seek out partners who unwittingly play out their dysfunctional past. This cycle becomes their present by re-creating multi-generational toxic shame.

It's a heavy load for any child, adolescent or young adult to carry.

Same Species, Different Brain

During his comical and highly entertaining video, *Tale of Two Brains*, marriage expert, minister and author, Mark Gungor, illustrates how a man's brain differs from a woman's. He places two brains on two podiums, one representing a man and the other a woman. His presentation to the audience is not only hilarious; it's chock full of fascinating content. He claims that men have an empty box in their brains, that *if* provided with the desired content, would be filled with empathy and heartfelt emotions. On the other hand, women have a box in their brain already filled to capacity with empathy and emotions.

When a woman tries to engage her male counterpart with these parts, the ones that come naturally with being a woman, the man, who is void of these inherent parts, can't automatically relate to or understand her needs and desires. They simply do not compute.

A simple solution—one of many, I'm sure, most any woman may conjure—probably seems like an impossible mission. But she will try to "convert" him, as if she thinks she is the one and only woman in the world who can. That's also in her DNA. But it doesn't work, just like it won't work when a woman thinks she can convert a gay man to be straight.

As a result, the battle of the sexes persists. A woman will remain frustrated until somebody can fill up the empty box of her man with the missing ingredients that do not automatically appear inside a man's brain. Some women can be patient with this and maintain reasonable expectations for their partner. Other women keep the bar perpetually raised too high and end up constantly disappointed. In my opinion, that's like expecting a man without legs to suddenly get up and walk or a cat to bark when someone is at the door. A miracle might create a new outcome, but since when are women, as amazing as we admittedly are, expected to be miracle workers?

Pets Have Feelings, Too

I have two dogs, Minnie, a 13-pound Shi Tzu, and Motik, a 13-pound Pekingese. Motik is short for Motik Shallee, which means "My Sweetie" in Hebrew. When we go for our walks, Minnie, a female, pees once. Motik, a male, seems compelled to pee on every blade of self-selected grass, every tree, every fire hydrant, every fallen leaf, every tire and every rolled-up newspaper. He marks his territory at least 15 times compared to the elegance of her one release. Motik shuffles, kicks and gyrates from side to side as if he were in a Zumba class. Our neighbors call him Fred Astaire. He just can't help it. He's a guy and can't help lifting his leg at least 15 times. It's in his nature, an essential part of his DNA. Minnie, who I've come to nickname Ginger Rogers, patiently waits for him or simply ignores what he's doing. I have to wait patiently for him to squirt as often as he likes until he feels satisfied. It's not rocket science. It's a male dog who needs to pee. For some reason, it makes him feel good, so what's the harm besides some wet grass, a few damp leaves and a soggy headline or two?

If women could accept the difference in gender as I do with my dogs, relationships would be so much easier. There would be no disappointment, disillusionment or bitterness. We seem to accept canine behavior easier than human behavior! Maybe if you remember that your man is also your pet, this philosophy will become more useful.

Just sayin' . . .

To assume that men don't have feelings is an erroneous assumption. They have decidedly strong feelings, including fears that they are out of touch with, or they are too frightened to admit how they feel, as it might make them seem like less of a man.

Men have needs exactly like women. There, I said it. They want to feel loved and respected. They want to matter, just like women. Unfortunately, they just have not learned the art of expressing themselves because they were shamed or not taken seriously when they tried it as children or again as a young adult.

This lack of communication creates a barrier in any relationship. She can't read his mind and he can't read hers. They unconsciously fear the same response they received as a child, but don't know it consciously, so instead they stay silent or act it out, often through anger of some kind. When this happens, the chasm grows wider. If both parties do take the time to learn each other's feelings and needs, their responses will change.

The bitch he calls his wife or partner can morph into a gentle, appreciative and loving woman. The husband, aka the asshole, can become engaging, empathic, supportive and understanding. It's a movable and flexible dynamic!

Consider this: does a husband drink because his wife nags him all the time or does a wife nag because her husband drinks too much?

It doesn't matter. Someone has to make a change. Either he stops drinking or she stops nagging. When this occurs, when they keep their eye on the prize and behave without unbearable tension and strife, their dynamic *will* change.

What Do We Do Now?

The Jewish philosopher Martin Buber maintained that humans are hard-wired for meaningful connections. He said that when we disconnect from each other we enter into crisis. The only way to overcome this is to learn how to reconnect. First, we must be willing to do so and then we have to agree to make the effort to see it through. You will find much more on learning how to reconnect in Chapter 10.

You may still be wondering why a man can't be more like a woman. Face it. They can't, unless of course they choose to stretch their emotional muscles and maximize their growth potential without feeling threatened that they will compromise or lose their masculinity, pride and/or ego. This might be a big ask for some and a real reach for others, but being open to perpetual possibilities and personal growth doesn't make a man any less of a man. In fact, it will make him *more* of a man as he becomes even more humane!

As for you women, dream big and be patient.

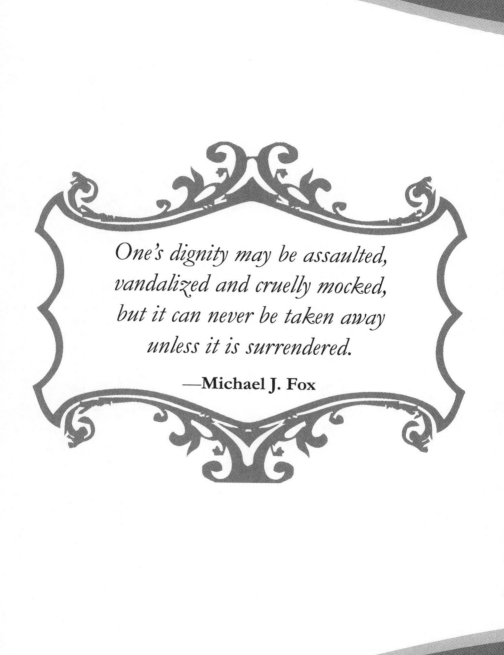

*One's dignity may be assaulted,
vandalized and cruelly mocked,
but it can never be taken away
unless it is surrendered.*

—Michael J. Fox

3

The Power of the Penis, the Patriarchy, Politics and the Pocketbook

When Shakespeare wrote, "Something is rotten in the state of Denmark," he could have easily expanded the list to Washington, D.C., Hollywood, California, Alabama, Minnesota, and New York, if not our entire nation. Why? Because since the dawn of time men in power feel that they have the right to abuse people, and in particular they feel entitled to commit sexual misconduct of all kinds. Whether it's Roy Moore, Harvey Weinstein, Bill Cosby, Charlie Rose, Al Franken, Anthony Weiner or any other high-profile celebrities, politicians, ex-presidents and our current president, occupying a powerful position does not give any of them the right to assault, batter, harass, grope or objectify women—at home, in the workplace or anywhere else.

Predators have many faces. They can be a politician, movie star, athlete, doctor, lawyer, judge, TV personality, businessman, professor, husband, boyfriend, father, grandfather, uncle, cousin, or neighbor. Any man, young or old, who feels that he has the right to take advantage of a child and/or woman without her consent, is a predator.

The further we go back in history the bigger the list gets. Today, with the explosion of social media, more and more men cannot get away with their behavior. We used to have no way to record the abominable behavior of powerful men, but we live in a different age now, which means the crimes and transgressions of more and more bad men can be revealed for the world to see. This is also due to how many women are finally standing up and raising their voices to say, "Enough is enough!" Our new heroines can be found in the halls of Congress, in boardrooms on Wall Street, and in courtrooms throughout the country. Kudos to those ladies for doing the right thing. They empower other women to stand up to their perpetrators and courageously share their stories.

How Does This Begin?

Early in life, usually long before we even know who we are, we fall in love, lose our minds, and make life-long commitments to men we may not even know very well. As we gaze into each other's eyes, our boundaries collapse and we think we have made a connection that will last forever. We are young, in love with love, and full of magical thinking, hopes, wishes, and dreams that we will live happily ever after—with this one special man.

"Till death do us part," we say in our wedding vows, unaware of how deeply we've been affected by our culture and the mythology of love. Ever since childhood, we've been inundated with songs of romantic love, heartbreak, co-dependency and loss, all of which support our myths.

"I can't live, if living is without you."

"It cost me a lot, but there's one thing that I've got, and its, my man."

"For whatever my man is, I am his forever more."

Each of us have our favorites, whether they have come to fruition or not.

Romantic movies usually feature happy endings, such as *Sleepless in Seattle, Love Actually*, and many more. Children grow up on Disney movies, which portray classic formulas we can only dream of: girl meets boy, boy meets girl, boy rescues girl, or girl falls in love with her hero or knight in shining armor and they live happily ever after. Girls grow into women, however, forever searching for their knight. News flash: the only knights available are wearing rusty armor.

We grow up believing in what has been projected on a screen or been heard in our music. We've been inundated with fairy tales and the stuff of dreams. We know that it just ain't so but something keeps us trying to make it happen, just like in a movie or a song or a book. Why is that? With more than 50 percent of marriages ending in divorce we know that living "happily ever after" is just a fantasy. As we mature, have children, and face responsibilities we didn't even know existed when we took our marriage vows, we realize that there is so much more to making love work than we knew or ever could have imagined when we were standing at the altar.

It's astounding how many people get married with little to no idea of what they are doing, or why. If only we could take some of the effort and money we spend on wedding planning and allocate it for pre-marital counseling—the world would be a better place. Preparation for any major life-changing event should be a requirement, but the thought of doing this never occurs to people, except those who ascribe to the essential codes of the Catholic religion. They make it mandatory for couples taking their vows to attend pre-marital classes. If only we could make it a federal law, especially for those under 30 years old! If only someone would tell all these innocent and naive boys and girls that their marriage is not going to play out like a Disney movie!

Harassment usually begins at home. It comes in many shades. It can be physical, emotional, verbal, sexual, intellectual and/or spiritual. Children who grow up in homes where harassment is a lifestyle will assume that it is the norm and mimic this behavior as they mature. When children are subjected to their mother being judged, criticized or abused, they will either identify with the abuser or the victim, but neither one are healthy choices. Sons will often model their fathers, while girls copy their mothers.

We only know what we know. As a result, this becomes multi-generational behavior until a therapeutic intervention of some kind can interrupt the cycle. In his book, *Healing the Shame that Binds You*, author John Bradshaw explains how multi-generational shame fosters each generation's behavior until somebody breaks the cycle.

To be fair, it's important to note that there are women who are attracted to and addicted to power. They seek out the attention of powerful men for their own aggrandizement. These predatory women pursue men of power to gain power of their own and are willing to sell their souls to the devil in order to accomplish it. The quintessential femme fatale, Scarlett, from *Gone with The Wind* used every man who could and would provide and satisfy her demands. She was ruthless, even stealing her sister's fiancé to secure lumber to rebuild Tara. Hers is an archetype that is universal and can be observed in every era and culture. Rita Hayworth portrayed this archetype in *Gilda* in the early 40s. She represented a beautiful woman seeking a powerful man to empower herself. In one of his more recent movies, *Blue Jasmine*, Woody Allen portrays Kate Blanchard as the modern-day Scarlett who doesn't have to think about tomorrow. She gets discharged from her marriage and is replaced by the next Mrs. Predator, leaving her in dismay, consternation and depression when she realizes that the devil was done with this dame.

The Cost of Addiction

I have met countless women in my practice who are not unlike cocaine addicts in their effort to find more powerful men with each new conquest, willing to pay whatever price they have to in order to land their man. As far as I can see, the cost *always* outweighs the gain. Men who are attracted to this archetypical female, invariably will find younger and prettier choices before too long. For many of these women, the high from conquering a man of power is worth the pain.

How does this begin? These conquests come from a lack of self-esteem, low self-worth and the search for finding a way to believe that they matter. Beneath this persona is usually a lost, wounded child, looking for love in all the wrong places. Healthy, evolved women would not be attracted to this kind of man. They hold themselves to a higher standard, while exemplifying a strong sense of self, coupled with dignity and self-respect. They would reject coupling with a man just to feel worthy as a woman. It's a matter of values and integrity that develops with a healthy, mature sense of self.

Water seeks its own level. Women use their sexuality to gain power in the same fashion that men use their power and pocketbook to conquer women. Similar to many addictions, this cycle becomes progressive and pervasive over time.

Margie's Myth

Margie was a woman who plowed through powerful men like Grant took Richmond in the Civil War. Each conquest was a trophy earning her the best that life had to offer as well as the worst. By the time she was 50 years old. Margie had struggled through three divorces, two live-ins and two prominent, successful boyfriends, all of whom lied and cheated on her. She had a knack for picking these guys out. When she came into my office she was with the last of these predatory men. Each had poked a bigger hole in her soul than the last. When she revealed their abusive behavior, I asked her why she allowed them to treat her in such an unflattering and degrading manner. Her answer was common. I have heard it many times from the partners of drug addicts and alcoholics.

"When he's not fuckin' around, he's wonderful. He treats me like a queen. He took me to Europe three times this year. He bought me some very expensive designer clothes, two Prada bags and much more. We're perfect for each other. We get along great and we have fun."

In Margie's case, it was the cheating that drove her mad.

"I give him my whole self. I am a great lover. We have amazing sex. I even suck his toes as well as his cock. We fall into each other's arms embracing throughout it with repeated lovemaking. Then the drama begins. He gets up to go to the bathroom. It's in the middle of the night that he's texting some other chick about their next rendezvous. I see it on his phone every morning. It's almost as if he leaves it for me to uncover."

"Really?"

I've heard this before from other women but I'm still astonished.

"How long has this been going on?"

"From the beginning, for the entire four years we've been together. I discovered it early on. He has many women, all over the world, that he uses for sex and entertainment. He says it means nothing. It's just a form of recreation for him, like gambling or spending a day at the races."

"How do you feel when you realize he has all these other women?"

"Terrible, like I don't mean that much to him. It makes me crazy and fills me with rage. One time, I actually pushed him into his closet and attacked him, punching him wherever my fist would land. I literally beat him up. I felt like I turned into a she-devil, someone I'm really not and don't like at all."

"Then why are you with him? What's your payoff or secondary gain for staying with someone who spends time with other women?"

Margie's story is sadly familiar. She is willing to lose her self-worth, self-respect, and dignity to keep this relationship alive. On top of that, she's putting herself at risk for a plethora of venereal diseases. But she won't let it go. For her, the pleasure is worth the pain. The highs are worth the lows. Each new conquest might double in its dollar value while each one that ends becomes more costly to her self-esteem. These patterns are eerily similar to most any addiction, and the behavior this requires is generated by the unconscious.

Margie is one of many I have counseled. When working through these case studies, the common denominator is always the same: low self-worth, shame and early childhood wounds from abuse, neglect or abandonment. In Margie's case, she made a decision long before she became an adult that she would never be poor again. The economic struggles she encountered in her childhood gave rise to her addiction to abusive men. But it wasn't as simple as that. Her father's failures to secure her safety as a child also contributed to her choices as an adult. The specific content is different with each case, but there is an underlying feeling of not feeling good enough for various reasons, each having to do with unresolved issues from their families of origin, and most of it is triggered by their fathers or another dominant male.

It is well-known that little girls get their self-worth from their daddies. It's part of the developmental process. When this doesn't happen, these girls grow up looking for what was missing when they were children; the need to feel they mattered, and the need to feel safe and secure. They act out their feelings in their adult life with a recapitulation to the past buried deep inside them. The resolution resides in treatment—and *not* in a man.

Beyond Money

Some women are attracted to powerful men for their status and accomplishments rather than just their bank account. These men are often well-respected pillars in the community—politicians, clergy, professors, and humanitarians. They appear to be virtuous, honorable men that no one would suspect had a bad bone in their body.

In Woody Allen's movie, *Crimes and Misdemeanors*, Judah Rosenthal is a pious Jew, philanthropist and philanderer , a man of high character and morals who also happens to be chief of ophthalmology at a large hospital in Long Island. To honor him for his outstanding service to the community, the hospital is dedicating a new ophthalmology center in his name. As the movie unfolds, we learn that Judah, who is married and planning his daughter's wedding, is not such a nice guy. He's been having an affair with a flight attendant, who after a few years pass, insists that he leave his wife and make a life with her. Her nagging and persistence makes Judah more and more uncomfortable. He tries to reason with her, console her and make her understand that a divorce is not possible. Unable to control her demands and outbursts, he hires a hit man through a sleazy network connected to his shady brother. The murder is committed and goes unresolved. After struggling with overwhelming shame and guilt, Judah eventually continues his life as if the killing never happened. His wife and daughter never find out, and his peers and colleagues maintain the belief that he is a man of substance, held in high regard by his colleagues and within the community. Woody Allen portrays the dark side of a man of piety and honor. In some ways, he may have been portraying the shadowy side of himself.

Women pursuing so-called honorable men are usually bright, well-educated, and successful in their own careers, but they are also seeking mental and intellectual stimulation, which means they need men who imbibe many of the same moral qualities and religious values as they possess. These women often meet a Dr. Jekyll, and soon learn that the man's alter-ego, his Hyde, is lurking in the shadows of the man they thought matched their standards.

This is not to say that men are exempt from this unexpected deception. They can be duped by unscrupulous women, too, but most men don't stick around if that becomes clear to them. Some do, however, and in that case most hope they will see a change in the woman's behavior over time.

Generally speaking, women are more patient and understanding than men. Women are usually the ones who drag the guy into couple counseling. As they sit, "pinned and wriggling on the wall," as T.S. Eliot wrote in *The Love Song of J. Alfred Prufrock*, men are more of a challenge than women when it comes to breaking down defenses and opening up to communicate in a genuine, meaningful way. At least that has been my experience.

Character defects linger without therapeutic intervention and sometimes never disappear even with it because the pay-off is too great to make any change. All too often, men are willing to lose the woman in exchange for their character defect. For them, it's just an addiction, with the drug of choice being conquering women. What remains so baffling is that so many of these accomplished, intelligent women continue to stick it out with these objectionable men.

Sarah's Lament

One day, a beautiful, bright and successful 54-year-old woman entered my office. Sarah had been in a rocky relationship with a man of power for nearly eight years. During their time together, he made it very clear that there would never be marriage or co-habitation. He made the rules and she sadly capitulated. It hadn't been like that in the beginning, though.

"The first night we met there were fireworks. We were introduced by a colleague of Sam's and the chemistry was off the charts. Sam couldn't wait to spend nights with me. It was on the second night after we met that he said, 'I want to get this right!' He wined and dined me, and took me to Italy only two months after we met. We shopped in the finest boutiques. He bought me beautiful clothes and fine jewelry and totally swept me off my feet. He introduced me to Italian art and all his favorite painters. I felt like a princess and fell madly in love. After we returned home, he placed a bottle of wine we had brought back from Rome on his kitchen counter. 'When you are certain,' he said, 'we'll open this and celebrate our commitment.'"

Sarah looked down during the entire time she shared her story with me. She was tearing up, and appeared to be heartbroken and in deep despair. She seemed to be in a state of disbelief that their relationship had so swiftly dissipated into merely dreams. Even worse, she realized that she had allowed it to linger to a point that was way past due. Once the conquest was over, her knight in shining armor morphed into the exact type of person she had been trying so hard to avoid. Sam became the jerk she never would have suspected. He disconnected, slowly but surely, pulling away each time he chose to go off and play golf, ride a bike, or partake in an activity that didn't include Sarah. She had walked away five times during the course of their relationship, only to surrender to his wishes each time he made an overture to reconcile. Each reunion would last less than a year, and the same behavior would once again rear its ugly head.

"Nothing changes until it changes," she told me. "I felt like I was in a merry-go-round relationship. I would have these heart-to-heart talks with Sam. He would be conciliatory, never defending his behavior, and then he would apologize before we parted. A few months would pass and I would hear from him again as if nothing had happened. It was so crazy."

Sam was a renowned neuro-surgeon and author, which was one reason Sarah was so attracted to him, and he traveled more than he stayed home. Born and raised in Santiago, Chile until he was 15 years old, Sam became a star soon after his family settled in Chicago. His good looks and Latin accent made him irresistible to the opposite sex and with age he became even more appealing. He excelled in everything. He was president of his high school class, a four-letter athlete and a scholar. His power did not stem from money. It was spawned from fame and charm.

Sarah told me that Sam was the most intelligent man she had ever known, a sort of Renaissance man, interested in art, literature, fine wine and writing, as well as medicine. He would hold court in social settings, and since he was such an authority on brain disorders, everyone was spell-bound when he spoke. He was invited all over the world to lecture at different medical conferences. He introduced Sarah to so many things she had rarely encountered. She had been so grateful for each experience he shared. However, their traveling together dwindled to occasional vacations, with him always choosing the destination, as he was rarely interested in where she wanted to visit.

I asked her why she continued to stay in the relationship once she realized they didn't want the same things and it became clear that her needs were not being met. Her pain was palpable.

"Honestly, I don't know. It's an addiction or co-dependency. I guess they're the same. I can't call it love, but I can't seem to let him go and he feels the same. Clearly he's not in love with me. Sam has never told me that he loves me. When I ask if he missed me when he's been away, his reply was always, 'No. I don't miss you when I'm gone. I have too many things to distract me, but I do enjoy you when we are together.' I don't understand why I continue to ask him the same question each time, as if he's going to change his answer. He has never introduced me to anyone as his girlfriend or significant other. I am always introduced as 'just Sarah' or 'Oh, this is Sarah.' It's so insulting and humiliating. It made me feel as if I don't matter. We haven't had sex in over a year. Sam says it's his prostate. He doesn't even kiss me or touch me. Occasionally, he takes my hand in a movie. He never looks into my eyes. He's hardly present. I can't believe I've settled for a loveless relationship. I could accept his diminished libido, but it's so painful to be deprived of closeness and connection. I have asked myself the same question many times. I find myself cursing under my breath when he turns everything around and blames me. My response is always muffled by his words and tone. Sam talks over me and I feel stupid and dismissed. I hang up the phone spewing, 'Fuck you!' He brings the worst out in me and I don't like it. It's not who I am!"

"Then what keeps you in the relationship? Surely it's not the money. You do very well on your own."

"I guess after almost eight years it's become the norm, a habit I can't break. The pain must be worth the pleasure. Sam's really a nice guy. He spends time talking to people all over the world he has never even met who have a brain tumor or some neurological disease. They search him out and he feels good when he is helping others.

He is nice to everyone—waiters, bell hops, children, even animals. It's so difficult to see the Hyde in him when he's Dr. Jekyll. It now feels like nearly eight years of my life have been wasted. I met Sam when I was 46 and I'm 55 now. What the hell is wrong with me?"

Sarah moved her hands to her forehead and began to sob.

"That was the way it was until it wasn't. One day, he accidently left his phone in my home. It rang and I picked it up by responding 'This is Sam's phone.' The caller abruptly hung up, but the screen showed a women's name and a city in another state. Moments later, a text arrived with a message that sent chills up my spine. A wave of nausea ran through me. Her message was a sex text, wondering when they could get together again. When I confronted Sam, he apologized, denying that he had ever participated. He told me she was someone from the past who he had not seen in years, a nurse who assisted him in the operating room. He asked for forgiveness, swearing that it never happened and he would not respond to any further communication she would initiate. Foolishly, I accepted his apology."

I waited for her to go on, pretty sure that it hadn't ended right then and there.

"But it didn't stop!' Sarah said. "It kept going and I could not accept this behavior. After the second time, I realized I had no choice but to end it. I had too much evidence to stay in denial. I told him about this quote, I don't recall who said it, but it was so apropos. 'Fool me once, shame on you. Fool me twice, shame on me.' Anyway, somehow, deep inside me, my soul would not rest unless I let go. I had lost respect and trust—for him, of course, but for myself, too. There was no way in hell I could maintain a relationship with a liar and a cheater."

Unlike Margie, Sarah felt being alone would be preferable to chronic disappointment. She didn't want to wake up each morning facing the truth about her hollow relationship. The ups were no longer worth the downs. The payoff was no longer worth the pain. Sarah reclaimed her self-worth and moved on with dignity.

Gabby Makes a Deal

A young beautiful widow named Gabby came to see me. She and her two teenaged children had been left with little money from her husband's death. He had committed suicide and his life insurance policy denied them any benefits. She took a job in sales in an exclusive department store, selling fine jewelry. She struggled to meet her debts and lived month to month until she met a man named Umberto.

One evening, while attending a musical at a local theatre, Gabby was immediately attracted to the conductor, whose passion and sensual expressions instantly commanded her heart. Immediately after the performance, Gabby found her way backstage to meet the man who had captivated her from the moment he lifted his arms to conduct the first notes of *Jesus Christ Superstar*. Umberto was Italian with all the accoutrements common to handsome men of that heritage, especially a conductor showing such leadership and command of others. The orchestra belonged to his baton and so it seemed, did Gabby.

That night began a romance, which would last more than 27 years.

Umberto traveled all around the world, conducting *Jesus Christ Superstar* with a traveling troupe, along with additional cast members he would audition wherever they were performing. Gabby traveled with him, attending most of his performances, and because Umberto had accrued a surplus of miles they usually flew first class. He moved into her apartment soon after both of her children went off to college. Umberto paid half of her rent and absorbed half the costs of all the living expenses, even though he was only living there less than half the time.

Gabby's life had taken a turn to economic security, but at a high price. Umberto was a womanizer. Wherever he conducted, women were seduced by his charm, his accent and his talent. They leaped at the chance to go to bed with him and he could not resist. He was the archetypal Don Juan and made no excuses to Gabby as she learned over time that there were many women in his life. They were his willful prey and there to stay.

"At first, I was devastated," she said, sounding as if she were in mourning. "I could not believe he had bedded so many women all over the world. I thought he was faithful and loved me. I never expected that he had someone wherever he performed. Worst of all, he never kept it hidden. It was as if he wanted me to know."

"How does that make you feel, knowing he has been with many other women?"

Gabby's response was no different than Margie's or Sarah's.

"Horrible! I feel like shit, like I'm just one of many, like a part of his harem. There is no exclusivity! I don't feel special, loved or important."

"Are you willing to continue knowing there are other women wherever he travels?"

Gabby didn't answer.

"Do you realize that in addition to chronic emotional pain you are also susceptible to venereal disease?"

She seemed to skip over my last question.

"I'm sure he is careful," she said.

I found her reply curious.

"Well, what's good for the goose is good for the gander," she said. "I can play the same game as him."

"Well, that's an option of course. But what about your feelings? How are you going to negotiate your feelings?"

"Ignore them," said Gabby. "I can have fun and find distraction just the same as him."

I saw her pain and sorrow. She was fighting back tears as she spoke.

"Why would you want to choose that path? You are young, smart and beautiful. Surely you can find another man who can make you feel like you matter. Every time you are confronted with another betrayal, your heart breaks a little more and that impacts your self-esteem. Life is too short to hang around men who suck the happiness out of you. You can do better Gabby!"

"You don't understand. I have a great life with Umberto. We have unbelievable sex together. All my expenses are covered. I travel all around the world first class and he is so exciting. I suppose the turn-on is worth the pain."

"Worth your broken heart and self-esteem?" I said. "Think about it. You are suffering from unrequited love. It's a prescription for pain."

"What kind of man am I going to find out there?" said Gabby. "All men are dogs, right?"

I remained neutral in that moment, for professional *and* personal reasons.

"At least I am financially secure and get to travel first class," she continued. "I know it's a bargain I'm making, but I don't see a better one out there. I really believe Umberto loves me, but it's love on his terms. It's the best he can do."

"Then why come to therapy? It sounds like you have made your decision."

"I needed someone outside of my friends and family to talk to. I don't tell my family anything. They don't need to know and I don't share this with my kids. "

"Think about how they would respond if they knew."

"That's exactly why I don't want them to know. I just want to share it with someone who won't judge me, with a person I can trust, like you. I didn't realize I would come to this conclusion on my own."

After a few months of counseling, Gabby opted for the deal she got from Umberto. I told her that if she really wanted to stay in the relationship she would have to accept the conditions and not allow his infidelity to break her heart. It was a deal she was making with the devil, but many women have been able to successfully pull it off, although I challenge how successfully. There's always a downside. If a woman can handle it, then she should stop complaining and move on. The right to self-determination is always a choice.

While this relationship would be untenable for some women, it was worth it to Gabby. She viewed the compromises she had to make, along with the pain and heartbreak she endured, as a fair trade for the 27 years they stayed together. A few months after she terminated treatment with me, Gabby passed away from lung cancer. I remain convinced that the relentless stress and intractable grief she endured may have been her executioner.

Angela's Ashes

One of the most tragic cases I have ever encountered in my professional career involves a woman named Angela. Born and raised in the Midwest as the younger of two girls, Angela was held hostage by her father for 43 years, initially programmed as a child to be his sex slave. Of course she was too young to understand his reprehensible behavior, and she kept it a secret, as her father commanded her to do. He brainwashed her into believing that they had a very special relationship and that it should be kept private between the two of them. Angela was obedient and subservient to the commands and wishes of her father, and the secret stayed with her until she managed to escape at the age of 43.

When Angela first came to me for therapy she had no memory of anything before the age of 17. She could not recall her father's sexual violations on her body that ultimately produced a dissociative disorder, along with stuttering. The silence he demanded through intimidation and obedience resulted in submissive behavior with all of her relationships. Silence became her default persona, while an internal rage damaged her spirit and self-worth. She had been allowed to attend school, but her father commanded Angela to return directly home immediately when the final bell rang, preventing her from any of the normal school activities and friends a girl might have. This restricted her social life to something nonexistent.

In spite of her father's persistent control and confinement, Angela developed a strong interest and talent for Tai Chi. Ironically, she was encouraged and supported by her father. She won many local, state and national competitions. It was her passion for Tai Chi that perhaps saved her life and sublimated her rage. Her father chaperoned her trips and managed her schedule. Her mother stood by like a ghost, denying that the sexual assaults perpetrated by her husband on their daughter had ever occurred. For 43 years, they lived in silent violence, each afraid to acknowledge their family secrets. Soon after Angela's older sister found her way out of the family household and shared that she, too, had been sexually assaulted by their father since early childhood, Angela, at the age of 43, finally escaped.

I sat in my chair horrified and in disbelief. I had heard about children who had been kidnapped and were forced to have sex with their captors, but I had never heard of a story like Angela's. She was desperate to find a semblance of recovery, and without even meeting me in person she had taken a huge chance and traveled a great distance to embark on this journey with me, as she wanted to see someone experienced in Inner Child Work. She had escaped her home and left the torture behind her, but it had followed her for another 12 years until at the age of 55, she miraculously showed up in my office.

Angela was so deeply shattered by the wounds her father had inflicted, and now she was on the edge of ending a relationship with a man. For five intensive days and nights, we hammered out her past. It took several days for her to recall instances in her early childhood where her father had forced her to have sex with him. She was just a child, five years old, when he first fondled her body and had her open her legs so he could put his finger into her vagina. He forced her to suck his penis, telling her that a child who loves her daddy would want to make him happy by kissing his penis, so he forced her little mouth around it until he would get an erection and ejaculate. Angela confessed that although this made her very uncomfortable, she would enjoy the feeling of him performing on her. Because she was so embarrassed to share her sexual arousal, she sobbed with guilt and shame.

The more Angela shared of her daunting past, the more she remembered. The rage she had been holding inside for so long was manifesting itself in her relationship with her lover, which meant that both of them were suffering the consequences of her past. The further we probed, the more her soft demeanor morphed into a raging bull. She screamed for the child she had left behind. She actually gave her lost child a voice, one she was never allowed to have.

As she crouched down on her knees on a mat in my office she held a bat over her head and stared frozen at the large pillows on the floor.

"I can't do this. I can't hit my father. Please, is there another way?"

"Bring it down on the pillow" I urged. "Put your father on the pillow and say what you couldn't say when you were so young and helpless. Tell him he stole your childhood and took away your innocence."

She sat motionless with the bat above her head, unable to bring it down as I instructed.

"Bring it down! Give him back the shame he gave you. Bring it down. He's right there!"

I continued to bellow these instructions while pointing to the pillow. It took some time, but finally, after hearing my voice in the background urging her to take back her life and give him back the shame that didn't belong to her, she took the plunge.

At first the bat came down softly, as if she were too hesitant to project her childhood voice and demeanor.

"More force!"

I shouted at her to bring the bat down on the pillow with more force.

"Just hit the pillow a few times and imagine he is coming into your room and sliding next to you in your bed. Reclaim your child! Save her!"

Angela stared at the pillow, still holding the bat over her head. Then all at once she shrieked the words she could never say as a child. She continued, because even as she developed into a teenager and a young woman, she had no voice—not until this moment in my office. She let loose, and once those words were unconstrained she no longer was bound by any fear or shame. Her voice penetrated the walls of the office, bursting through time and space, as they freed her from the physical, emotional, and spiritual bondage of her past.

"I hate you! I hate you! You destroyed my life, you scum bag, son of a bitch, piece of shit. How dare you! How dare you! You took away my childhood. You stole my innocence, you bastard. I hate you, I hate you, I hate you!"

Angela howled on and on, cursing her father over and over, as she continued to heave, nearly breathless, pounding the bat with an energy and force that was clearly foreign to her. She unleashed the rage that had been locked in her belly for a lifetime.

After each episode and outburst, I directed her to hold her inner child. I placed a teddy bear in her arms, symbolizing her inner child, and provided the words, a few at a time, which had been denied to her when she was a child—words that would finally provide her with the validation she had never experienced.

"It's not your fault, Angela. It's not your fault."

She muttered the words softly to the teddy bear.

"You were precious, perfect, lovable, and innocent—a child of God."

Once again, she repeated my words.

It wasn't your fault.

These words seemed to stick with her a minute before she could repeat them.

"You didn't deserve this, Angela, and from now on, I am going to take care of you."

She looked at me and I nodded, a silent reminder that she was her own ultimate caretaker.

"I will take care of you forever, and of all the people you are going to meet, I am the one who will never abandon you."

Tears fell on to Angela's cheeks as she heard the words that began to heal her soul. She repeated these words, supplementing them with her own to help her inner child heal from the years and years of wounds, which had been inflicted upon her by her father.

The first man in her life who she trusted had committed acts of sexual violence all through her life until she could no longer bear the pain. Her escape had been planned. She managed to slip out of the house in the middle of the night, never to return again.

The wounds of the child remain until a corrective experience occurs. Although the treatment was demanding and painful, it had to be done. By breaking through the wall of repression and amnesia to discover her truth, Angela was finally on her way. I encouraged her to write her story, to make it known to others who had experienced a similar traumatic injustice. She eventually self-published a book, which led to her psychological and spiritual freedom.

Abuse in Common

In her book, *The Drama of the Gifted Child*, Alice Miller writes that it is not just the action alone that makes us sick. It is the repression and keeping of a secret that keeps us sick.

In ordinary, everyday relationships, we still see power struggles, perhaps not as violent or newsworthy as Angela's, but painful still to both men and women. A healthy relationship is never based on power. It is egalitarian by nature. The power in a relationship exists in the relational space where the couple resides—not in one or the other. What makes the space healthy is being present and connected, seeing each other with new soft eyes and an open heart, and all the while learning the landscape and language of each other.

Marcel Proust once said, "The real voyage of discovery consists not in seeking new landscapes, but in having new eyes."

Margie, Sarah, Gabby and Angela are women who suffered from emotional and spiritual abuse. All were successful in their own right. Each earned a substantial amount of money. Margie believed it was never enough, which was caused by the insatiable wound of her childhood. Sarah felt that her self-worth was more important than her legendary boyfriend. Gabby made herself a martyr and a victim of her own choices in life. Angela was finally liberated.

Many women who are physically abused, battered and sexually assaulted choose to stay in relationships, regardless of black eyes, broken bones and scarred faces. Sleeping with the enemy is a common phenomenon in our culture. All are considered to be a love addiction. These women are addicted to their abuser, due to low self-esteem and a fear of abandonment. Some are fearful of leaving, due to unimaginable consequences they can't seem to cope with or accept.

Although this book is not essentially about abuse, it is important to note that according to domesticviolencestatistics.org, figures indicate that at least one in every three women worldwide have been beaten, coerced into sex or otherwise abused during their lifetime. Most often, the abuser is a member of their own family. What seems most astounding is that each day in the United States more than three women are murdered by their husbands or boyfriends.

With the exception of Angela, all the other women were addicted and self-imprisoned by their captors—the men they *chose* as partners. None of them were victims. Margie, Sarah and Gabby each had a choice. Angela was held hostage through intimidation and obedience.

The power was different in each man. Margie's partner had enormous wealth, Sarah and Gabby's partners had position and fame, and Angela had a commanding, controlling and formidable father. Each woman capitulated to their oppressor for their own reasons. Each paid an enormous price. Angela of course had no options. Margie, Sarah and Gabby each *chose* their partners unconsciously to teach them a very important lesson they needed to learn.

Unfortunately, they didn't have the opportunity to work as a couple to discover the lesson and reap its benefits. It takes both partners to make the commitment to work through any underlying issues. However, individually, they at least could see that the fantasy they projected did not match up with reality. Each *chose* their own path based upon knowing if the consequences were worth it.

Once again, they chose their own fate.

Perhaps all of these woman could have benefited from reading the words of Hamlet, as written so eloquently by William Shakespeare.

"To be, or not to be, that is the question:
Whether 'tis nobler in the mind to suffer
The slings and arrows of outrageous fortune,
Or to take arms against a sea of troubles
And by opposing end them. To die—to sleep,
No more; and by a sleep to say we end
The heartache and the thousand natural shocks
That flesh is heir to: 'tis a consummation
Devoutly to be wish'd. To die, to sleep;
To sleep, perchance to dream—ay, there's the rub:"

What Do We Do Now?

All of this relationship work is a process, not a one-time event. It needs to be taught and integrated because there is no handbook provided when we fall in love. It's so interesting that when one wants to learn an instrument, play a sport, drive a car and so on, there are lessons to go along with the activity and some of them even require a test you must pass before you can fully indulge. Yet, marriage and parenting, perhaps the two most important investments we make in our lives, we know least about and require no litmus test of any kind. Wouldn't a course in making love work be a good idea? Perhaps a course in "The Power of the Penis, the Patriarchy, Politics and the Pocketbook" would do many women—and men—a lot of good.

*The most common way
people give up their power
is by thinking they don't have any.*

—**Alice Walker**

4

The Dangers, Drags, and Dubious Dregs of the Dating Game

Dating in the 21st century is not for sissies! Consider yourself lucky if you're not stuck inside all of that chaos, but if you are, keep reading! The dating world can be disastrous at any point, but when a relationship grows over time and you become fully vested in a guy, what do you do when he suddenly decides he wants out?

"It's not about you; it's about me!"

Sound familiar?

Of course this comment is even worse when your man goes MIA in a marriage or a long- term relationship, but even in the context of dating it can be debilitating. When you confront your dating partner with feelings of abandonment or detachment , what does he do? He either denies his behavior, which makes you feel like you're crazy, or he fesses up, admitting that he's not feeling the way he felt when your relationship began. You ask yourself, "Is it me? Have I changed?" "What have I done wrong?" You tell yourself that you are the same person you were a year ago, except that you are a year older. Confused and bewildered, you second-guess your-self, develop a sudden case of insecurity, and a new set of feelings that you no longer matter. "What did I have then that I don't have now?" More than likely, the worst part is, you'll be left on your own to try and answer these questions because Mr. It's Not About You It's About Me will be long gone. In that case, the first favor you can do for yourself is to stop blaming yourself and choose to *not* be a victim, especially not because of him, whoever he is, who could simply not commit.

The Bait and Switch, the Hit and Run, and the Seven-Year Itch vs. the Seven-Week Dude

In the context of relationships, these terms take on different meanings than the common definitions we find in the dictionary.

Hit and Run is a term used primarily in auto accidents; however, it can be easily applied to the dynamics of a relationship, particularly in its beginning stages.

Bait and Switch is a form of fraud commonly used in retail sales when customers are baited by merchants advertising products or services at a low price, but when customers visit the store or website they discover that the advertised goods are not available or the customers are pressured to consider similar, but higher priced items. This term is also applicable to describe what happens during the first stage of a relationship.

Picture this: you think you've met one terrific man, but then you turn the corner and suddenly, without warning, out comes his polar opposite. You've suddenly entered the world of Dr. Jekyll and Mr. Hyde. In the beginning, Dr. Jekyll presents himself as a charming, well-intended potential partner. He's present, asks the right questions, and showers you with affirming comments, making you feel that he is genuinely interested in getting to know you. His gentle kiss when you say goodnight leaves you with a warm, fuzzy feeling, and when he says let's do this again or promises that he'll call you, it sounds for real, so you go home filled with excitement and hope—until he never calls and you're left alone to wonder why.

Throughout many years of my practice I have heard many women tell me similar stories of dating disasters, some of which took a long time to manifest themselves, for as we know, it can often look rosy in the beginning, during the honeymoon phase, before other realities set in. Here are a few examples of the follies of our so-called "meaningful" relationships.

Janice and Alex

They were introduced through a mutual friend when she was 58 and he was 59, but neither one of them knew each other's age. The moment they met. Alex showered Janice with compliments, which were soon followed with promises. He played her like a Stradivarius, enticing her into his larger-than-life existence. Strangely, Alex never asked her age, although he later admitted that he believed Janice to be in her forties. Janice, beguiled with Alex's methods of seduction, fell deeply in love with both him and the lifestyle he offered. He convinced her to move into his 8,500 sq. ft. mansion on the water overlooking Biscayne Bay, one of the most exclusive neighborhoods in Miami Beach. No home in that area was worth less than ten million dollars. Wide-eyed and bushy-tailed, she accepted his offer.

A successful professional, Janice took a leap of faith and was persuaded by Alex to sell her apartment, which she did before moving into his home, believing that "this is it—I've finally found my one true love!" She had been through two failed marriages and a few long-term relationships, including a five-year live in affair. At this point in her life, Janice was no novice when it came to relationships. One would think that an intelligent, self-made woman, approaching the age of 60, with an abundance of life experience, would have given up on the fantasy of finding a dream man. But like many bright middle-aged woman, only six years away from Medicare, fantasy can still trump reality and the lure of the Disney prince still reigns, at least enough to make women like Janice sell their home and move in with a man they really don't know that well. She was one of many blissfully unaware that she was selling her soul to the devil. Janice lost herself in the promises of a man she knew for less than six months.

Alex had been married twice, had two children who were grown and lived away on their own, and appeared totally smitten with Janet, until the day she announced that her son and daughter-in-law were going to have a baby, making her a grandma for the first time. It was then, coupled with their first international trip, when Alex discovered Janice's real age. In no time, he began to withdraw from their relationship. It was subtle at first, but Janet soon felt him becoming more and more distant and wondered what had caused such a shift. When she confronted him about her feelings, he dismissed it as not being true, and blamed it on her insecurities. Alex never admitted his feeling of disappointment with her age and that she would soon have a grandchild. He pretended to keep the relationship alive, but all the while he was having an affair, unbeknownst to Janet, who still believed he was faithful and in love with her.

It didn't take much longer before Alex's behavior morphed from an authentic interest and connection into a more obvious estrangement and aggression. He no longer showered Janice with the compliments he once had. He became hostile and easily irritated with her, without cause or provocation. Their once fulfilling sex life became much less satisfying, bordering on barren. When Janet tried to communicate her feelings, Alex stonewalled her, which made her feel intimidated and quite unable to express herself. Confused, bewildered and rejected, she continued to believe that their relationship was intact and that perhaps Alex had been correct in his interpretations regarding her insecurities.

Self-doubt and suspicion soon replaced contentment and joy.

By then, Janice and Alex had been living together for nearly three years, traveling and maintaining their normal social engagements. Alex had several personal and business issues that infiltrated their relationship, contaminating what was once their sacred space. Janet tried to support his concerns with her experience and knowledge as a psychologist , which she had been for more than 25 years. It all fell on deaf ears. The more she tried to console him, offering suggestions and viable options, the more defensive and combative he became. Alex's judgments, fault-finding and criticism became pervasive, until one Tuesday evening he told Janice he was not happy, had not been happy for a year, and wanted her to leave, giving her until that Friday to get out.

Janet was stunned. She was clueless, not knowing what had happened to cause such a sudden dismissal. She confessed that she had been aware of the shift in their connection, but she didn't realize he had been unhappy with her. He had disguised his feelings so well that learning he had not been happy for a year shocked her. They had just returned from a great weekend, sharing time with friends and her family. Janet assumed it was the stress Alex was having with his business and his adult children, mainly his daughter, who had always felt contempt for him, due to her unresolved childhood issues.

Janice moved out, according to Alex's wishes, without anywhere to go. A friend offered her an apartment until she found her own. Overwhelmed with grief and unexpected loss, Janice fell ill, aching from a broken heart, which soon morphed into diabetes. Her life had been shattered along, with her self-esteem. She was now approaching 62 years of age, alone and basically homeless. She never suspected that on Saturday, just one day after she left Alex's mansion on North Bay Road, that another (younger) woman would move into what had been Janice's safe haven for three years, abruptly taking over her closet and enjoying all the furnishings and housewares, which Janice had chosen to create the home she and Alex had shared for those years.

As soon as she heard about this, Janice made an appointment to see me. After listening to her story, I told her about another person I had treated for something similar.

Mindy and Jack

The night Mindy and Jack met through a mutual friend felt like a time warp for both of them. Mindy, a bright and beautiful woman in her late 50s, and Jack, who was a few years older, but not yet retired, felt an instant attraction for each other.

"I want to get his right!" he told her on their second date, which was the very next night.

"Me too," Mindy said, full of the same high hopes she once had with her first love, many years earlier.

They both agreed not to jump between the sheets until they learned a little more about one another, giving time a chance to do its thing. It wasn't long before their hearts collided and they were off to Italy to celebrate Mindy's 60th birthday.

Jack was an investment banker who had raised his two children as a single parent. His ex-wife had been determined to remain incompetent, leaving him with sole custody of their children. His work carried him all over the world, however, which made it difficult for him to manage both fatherhood and a career. Both had been sacrificed along the way, but in spite of his time constraints and traveling, his children grew up to become successful adults and were his pride and joy.

When Jack met Mindy, he had quite a full life. In addition to his consulting work, which took him around the world, he had also written several books on the art of business and investment counseling and was in the midst of doing more. He was well-respected and world-renowned in his field. He had a love of the arts, theatre, ballet, concerts and opera. Like Sam, the renowned neurosurgeon you met earlier, Jack might also be considered a Renaissance man, which delighted Mindy to no end, just like how Sarah once responded to Sam. She fell head over heels for him and he returned the affection, so she assumed he felt as if their relationship was "the real thing." He wined and dined her and couldn't get enough of her, physically and sexually.

Mindy thought she had won the lottery. In addition to all his charms, he was considerate, gracious and very generous, bestowing her with gifts she could never afford.

"I couldn't believe this man was for real. He's handsome, brilliant, humble, sexy, sophisticated and worldly. I can't imagine what he might have seen in me. He was also philanthropic, great with my family, and loved to have fun. He played golf when he wasn't traveling or on a lecture tour, and rode his bike for hours, sometimes as much as 50 miles. He swam as often as he could. I can't say enough about his character, which right from the start I was convinced was authentic and good-natured, that is until it slowly disappeared over the nine years we were together. Everything—it all disappeared!"

Mindy's head fell into her hands as the tears spilled down her cheeks, smearing her eye liner and mascara. She wiped them over and over, taking turns blowing her nose and pouring her heart out.

"Nine years!" she said. "Can you imagine? I was in a fucking trance for nine years—and I never did anything that I knew could have caused him to change his feelings and behavior. He pulled away slowly. I was so unsuspecting. It never occurred to me that he might be having an affair, or that he even had an issue with me. He often found fault for the silliest reasons."

"Give me an example," I said.

I wanted to understand Mindy's perception of what she considered to be silly.

"Well, once time when I asked for an umbrella when we were out in the rain he became annoyed and criticized me for not wanting to get my hair wet. They were stupid reasons—the dumbest things—like putting on lipstick at the table when we were in a restaurant or shaming me for wanting to get something to eat when I was hungry and he was entertaining his grandchildren. They were things I couldn't understand in the moment. It was as if he were trying to find reasons to withdraw. It worked because his words of devotion and affection changed from 'you are loved, and adored,' or 'you are precious,' to nothing. He no longer said he loved me, and when I asked him if he missed me when he was away, he said, 'Well, now that you mention it, I like the solitude when I'm away. It gives me time to think.' My heart sank when he said that. It was clear that he no longer wanted the relationship. We broke up six times during our nine years together, and he always took the initiative to come back to me. It was like a dance. 'Come here. No, go away.' I never knew how he really felt. Our love-making stopped completely, and when I tried to talk to him, about it I got one word responses."

A long pause was followed by an even longer sigh. Mindy wiped her eyes, now swollen and red, and leaned back and curled her legs under her.

"What's the use? It's done. He's gone and is probably relieved. His first intentions faded over time as the intimacy began to grow. I guess he was just another dude afraid of intimacy."

I handed Mindy another box of tissues. I had heard this monologue innumerable times and learned to keep a full supply of Kleenex in my office. In this case, Mindy's details were different than Janice's but the structure always remained the same.

It was a dance of codependency. I call it the "come here, go away," two step. I have counseled countless women who share the same heartbreak. My office had soaked up thousands of tears over the years. They cry me a river with their heartbreaking stories of disappointment and unwarranted rejection, and most never see the train coming, let alone the wreckage.

Understanding their shortcomings and fears of intimacy never seems to matter to these women. Hit and run or bait and switch both produce an emotional affect that leaves a deep wound, which often requires years of recovery. The scars left behind can often be triggered during future relationships, leaving post-traumatic stress disorders all over the place, including a slew of them on miscellaneous dating sites.

A broken heart with broken dreams has no intellect or wisdom. It resides in the limbic system, only feeling pain and loss.

Mindy's parting words that day when she left my office have stayed with me for a long time, and they probably will forever. In fact, she was the one who inspired the title of this book when she said, "I hate him. I hate that bastard! I hate the man I love, and I don't know what to do about it."

Seven-Week (Weak) Men

We cannot discuss the debacles of dating and relationships without including the "seven-week (weak) men" syndrome. During the entire span of my private practice there seems to be a theme that keeps reappearing, with women meeting men, online or otherwise, beginning a relationship with all the makings of success, only to have it end abruptly at the seven-week mark.

This is not too different than the "seven-year itch," when people (mostly men) seek a relationship outside of their existing one at around the seven-year mark. Seven-week men check out after the conquest is confirmed, which usually takes place just short of two months. Some of these men are married, looking for a distraction from their boring marriage, while others are surfing for a short tryst that will satisfy their sexual needs, but those urges often seem to fade within seven weeks. Others may wig out when they realize that the woman they have "conquered" has fallen in love and expects a real commitment, something that never seems to occur to the man involved, from the get-go to the end. For most, if not all of these men, the fling was strictly meant to satisfy their ego because conquering a woman always seems to make them feel more powerful as a man.

Millie and Jason

These two met in a Whole Foods market. The moment they laid eyes on each other, sparks flew. It was as if they had known each other from a different lifetime.

"He was smitten from the moment our eyes met," Millie told me.

"What happened to suddenly change things?"

"I really don't know. Something in him, for sure, because he made special plans to take me out for my birthday and brought over several gifts. He said I looked beautiful, and then he kissed me and brought me close to him, telling me how much he loved me. We embraced for a moment before he continued. 'There is something I need to tell you, Millie,' he said. 'This is not easy, and I know it is going to hurt you, but I can't see you anymore.' I freaked out. 'What!?!' I was shouting, which is out of character for me, but he shocked me. 'Seriously?' I said. 'You're joking, right?' Jason stood there silently, without saying a single word. He just crouched over me while I sat frozen on the sofa. 'Don't ask me to explain,' he told me. 'I can't. It's not going to work for me. It's not you. I love you—you're special; I mean, you're a blessing for any man."

I listened to Millie, already saddened to know that she was hardly the only woman who's been through something like this. I nodded for her to continue.

"You can't even give me a reason?' I said to him, trying to hold my tears back. I was so sad in that moment, and I felt so angry and even had actual physical pain. In that moment, I wasn't able to define the myriad of feelings that were shooting through me like a torpedo."

Even now, weeks later, Millie still writhed in discomfort as she disclosed her heartbreak.

"Why would someone who claimed he loved me, leave me so suddenly, without any cause or explanation? Why!"

I had no response that would alleviate her pain, no answer that would make sense. Jason was not my client so there was no reason to project my thoughts onto him. I am not a mind reader, but Millie's story was certainly not new to me. She was not the first woman to share this tale of woe and most likely not the last. I had heard it many times—boy meets girl, they fall in love—boy leaves girl for little or no apparent reason, and girl falls apart. In many cases, the girl gets pregnant, either aborts or has the child, without sharing the information with the father, and the child grows up, fatherless, forever wondering about the identity of his or her father.

The cascade of emotions that flow through these women in my office leave scars that may be irreparable. When this becomes a pattern, it is imperative to try to understand *why* they feel an attraction to a man who can't commit. Why do we unconsciously keep repeating the same choices? The father of psychoanalysis, Sigmund Freud, called it "repetition compulsion," while psychiatrist and author Alice Miller refers to it as "the logic of absurdity." Whatever you choose to call it, this cycle is something to be reckoned with!

A woman has to explore why she does what she does.

Why Do We Keep Repeating the Same Mistakes?

All women need to understand that this behavior is not a coincidence, but a pattern that keeps repeating itself, trying to work out some unfinished business from the past. Where does this madness come from, and why? The reasons are plentiful, but the common denominator is childhood wounds. Since we choose our mates both consciously and unconsciously, it is imperative for us to examine the reasons. Otherwise, change can never occur.

This is how multi-generational shame is handed down from one generation to the next. The pattern of always looking for love in all the wrong places continues, no matter what name we might call it, whether it's codependency, the most common label attached to it, or a simple combination of bad judgment, desperation, or plain old stupidity.

One of my favorite examples of the seven-week exploitation cycle was presented to me by a woman named Julie, who came to see me soon after her split from her last boyfriend of exactly seven weeks. The way in which she presented the story to me could easily have been made into a short novel. Her experience had left such a jolting impression upon her that she had chosen to write the story with the intention of turning it into a novel. She brought her meanderings, reflections and thoughts into our session. She actually had a bound manuscript with her and had completed the first part, which she titled it, *The Illusion of Love: An Internet Disaster.*

I wanted to hear every word of it, although time would not permit it, as reading 89 pages would have taken way too long. She did however share the most salient parts so I could get an accurate impression of her experience. Julie was an excellent writer, and I was fascinated not just by her story, but how she presented the information.

Sydney, 65 years old and married, was seeking excitement as a distraction from his compulsive workaholic nature. He and his wife were separated but still married. She lived in Chicago while he was in Miami. He was with his buddies one day when they told him about internet dating, something he didn't know much about.

"But technically I'm married and really not available," he said.

"Well, you are alone, Syd," one of his friends said, "and it will give you a diversion from all your work. You don't have to get serious. Just have some fun."

Sydney was an intellectual person, a powerful entrepreneur and a successful developer. He took up his friends' suggestion without hesitation, believing it would be an innocuous, innocent sport, just for his amusement. He had absolutely no intention or interest in developing a relationship with anyone. He just wanted to have fun.

Julie, on the other hand, a bright, beautiful and rather innocent woman in her early 60s, was seriously looking for a relationship. She had been divorced, three times, and had three grown children and five grandchildren. She was a successful recruiter for a large investment company and had lived alone for several years, and was eager to find the right man as a life partner. She joined a dating site, hoping that she might find an appropriate mate who could fill her needs and desires.

One evening, quite late in fact, Julie pulled into her driveway with a sense of weariness. She opened the gate to the courtyard, ignoring the cascading sounds of recycled water pouring endlessly from the statue of the Water Lady, perched upon a Roman fountain. When she turned the key and opened her front door, Danny Boy, her 12-pound Maltese, was overjoyed to see her. He jumped up against her skirt, wiggling his tail relentlessly, until she picked him up and kissed him hello. After searching the refrigerator, hoping to find something she had missed in the morning, she settled for a soda and a few pretzels and headed toward her office. Her day had been long, arduous and filled with complaints and endless telephone calls. Julie was beginning to appreciate the peace and tranquility single life and solitude could offer. Although being alone was not her first choice, she was beginning to think that the serenity it offered might be worth it. She slipped off her heels, sat down in front of her Dell computer and clicked on her server, hearing a familiar sound.

"You've got mail!"

Julie had received an unexpected response to her online dating profile. She glanced down until she saw the J-date email, clicked the link, and viewed the new messages of interested suitors. They were all so homogenous that it was difficult to distinguish one from the other. Nothing original, she thought. Even worse, the men were either unattractive or barely presentable. Several had no photos and she hated that. How could anyone expect a response without at least a photo? Her photo was there for the world to see. Strangely, against her normal impulses, she chose to ignore them all, except the one without a photo.

Good evening Lady Julie,

I want to know what you ache for and if you dare to dream of meeting your heart's desire? I want to know if you will risk looking like a fool for love, for your dream and for the adventure of being alive? We have a great deal in common, and a fair amount in distinction of each other. Would you be willing to communicate and explore the avenues that beckon us to travel on together?

Sydney

Julie told me that she considered ignoring the message.

"After all," she said, "there was no photo, and worse yet, his brief profile revealed that he was separated. There was nothing else he offered. I had promised myself never to date 'never married' or separated men. I felt it was a sure bet for future problems. I mean, there was always the chance that their marriage could be reconciled, or they were online surfing for an interruption from their mundane lifestyle. On top of that, he mentioned nothing about himself in his profile, except that he was separated. It's amazing how an in-complete profile could have elicited a response from me like it did. I guess the mystery was seductive, especially after reading his first entry."

By then, the tears were rolling down Julie's cheeks and I of-fered her some tissues. I couldn't help relating to her. Many of my own love-life experiences matched hers. Naturally, I wanted to hear more. I was fully aware of the counter-transference that was emerging, but I kept the session clean, just listening with great awareness.

Julie continued to read from her manuscript.

Dear Sydney,

Your email was titillating and very seductive. I felt compromised by not being able to see your photo or learn more about you. Your profile is empty. You have the advantage of viewing both my photo and my profile. Yours is like a skeleton. How can you expect anyone to learn anything about you and decide if there's any common ground? Perhaps you might be willing to consider filling in the gaps.

Julie

This communique went on for several weeks until they finally met. He referred to her as "Cinderella" in all his emails and began signing them as "Prince Froggie." He assured her that she would not be disappointed. His writing style sizzled for her and she was off to the moon on gossamer wings, creating the future of her life with this exciting man, who continued to shower her with Robert

Browning-esque poetry with his enticing emails, luring her to finally accept a date after three weeks of emailing.

Julie's hunch wasn't wrong. Sydney drove up in a new premiere Jaguar, and when he entered her home he dazzled her with his looks and style. He was everything she had hoped he would be—brilliant, handsome, rich and seemingly smitten with her.

What more could a woman ask for?

He opened the door of what he called his "carriage" for her and as Julie entered Sydney pointed out that there was a gift on her seat, a small box, perfectly gift wrapped. Julie felt excited, like a little girl. Her giddiness in just relating the story made it sound as if it were just happening to me. I was totally absorbed and swept away with her tone and affect. I could identify with my own experiences. How many times had I found someone who met my criteria and expectations for a partner, who had the same presentation, and then disappointed me profoundly as he disappeared into the night, like a ghost?

Julie was certainly not the only client I could compare notes with because there have been many, but her presentation took me onto a wavelength, which made me have to concentrate extra hard to remain mindful and to stay present as her counselor, instead of her commiserating girlfriend, a distinction I always have to remember.

When she opened the gift she stood paralyzed with excitement as she saw the Limoges statue of a prince, dressed in full regatta, holding his arm out with a glass slipper. My mouth joined hers—fully agape. We were both sharing the same experience in wonder and delight.

Things took off and continued to move along for the next few weeks. Julie's heart was filled with love and excitement. Syd not only showered her with gifts each time they saw each other; he also confessed how much he loved her and wanted to spend his life with her—until he didn't. The charade lasted seven weeks, and with each week he seemed to develop deeper and deeper feelings and commitment.

Syd introduced Julie to his business partner when he took her to see his office, which was filled with all his art holdings, covering most of the walls. His developments were pervasive, including the entire country, from New York to California and South Florida. Julie had fantasies of giving up her work and living a life of luxury, as Syd had intimated it would be on more than one occasion. Her excitement was only transcended by her love for this amazing man who had swept her off her feet.

But the dream ended abruptly and the nightmare began. It was exactly seven weeks from the day she received her first email. Syd came to Julie's home, as he had done several times before. They watched a movie, *Frida*, which explored themes of fidelity and loyalty. When it was over, so was their romance—terminated by Prince Froggie, as he realized he had taken his romance with Julie too far and had no way to escape, except to say good-bye to his Cinderella.

Julie's hopes, dreams and expectations dissipated into thin air, along with the man she thought would be the one who would take her to a castle where they would live happily ever after.

"You would think that by now, at the age of 62, I would know better. I think it's time I gave up the fantasy."

I looked at Julie and nodded, but I also made the same decision for myself.

What Do We Do Now?

It's not easy to change the neuropathways created by Disney and the movies we have grown up with during our childhood. They leave such an indelible mark in our psyches. Our beliefs are formed early on and abandoning them is not an easy process. The mirror neurons in our brain allow us to mimic both good and bad ideas and values. Being raised to believe that "someday my prince will come" is a message that is nearly impossible to erase. It follows us at any age, and thinking we have outgrown such an influence is something we do at out our own risk.

My advice? Enjoy the movies, by yourself, with your children and/or grandchildren, or even on a date, but remember—it's a movie! It's not real life! The only prince who is going to show up in your life is animated, and the only horse you may encounter leaves his shit on the ground for you to step in, so watch your step!

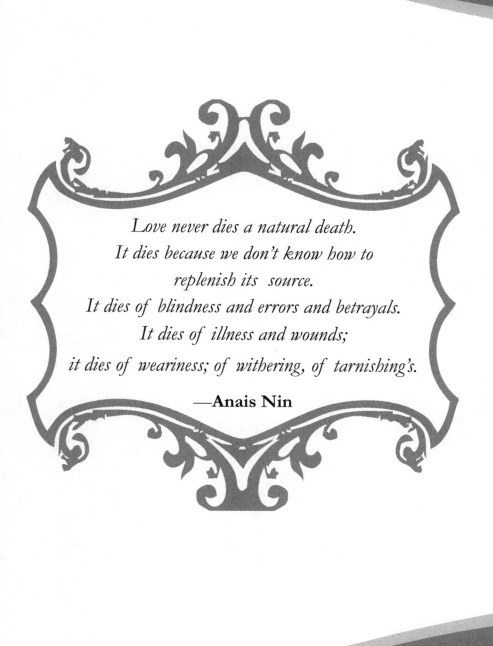

Love never dies a natural death.
It dies because we don't know how to
replenish its source.
It dies of blindness and errors and betrayals.
It dies of illness and wounds;
it dies of weariness; of withering, of tarnishing's.

—Anais Nin

5
Don't Fix It! Just Listen!

Men seem to assume that when a woman bounces a concern or a statement of fact off of her male partner he is automatically responsible to fix it. For example, if she simply states that the air-conditioner is on the blink, it immediately elicits a response of annoyance or anger.

"Why can't you take care of it? Why is it always my job?"

God knows why men respond this way, when all their female partner is doing is sharing the fact that the air-conditioner is not working. Unfortunately, his response leaves her wondering why he looks so cross as he screws up his face and rolls his eyes.

"I called the service company," she'll say," and they are coming out tomorrow."

This is just one example of how men too often respond to something that sounds like a request or a demand instead of a simple statement of fact.

Why do men feel obligated to fix the problem when all the woman wants is for him to listen and share in the truth of the situation? Men are not alone in this conflict. Women often respond the same way, although, in fairness, not nearly as often.

The Gift of Active Listening

Perhaps the reason for all the misunderstanding boils down to one other simple fact:

Listening is a skill, a learning process that requires mindfulness and practice.

Effective communication, which begins with active listening, is perhaps the most essential ingredient in any successful, conscious relationship. Sadly, it is also something that most couples lack and seem to take for granted.

Most couples think talking trumps listening, which is not true. Learning how to be present and listen is paramount in any relationship. Men assume too often that when there is no intention or request by the woman that he is free to wander—in his mind.

I saw this first-hand while I was sitting next to a couple on a flight who were returning from their vacation. The woman was perusing through an airline magazine, which was filled with vacation destinations they featured as part of where they traveled.

"Look honey, this looks like a great vacation spot," she said.

Without any provocation or expectation, her husband responded in an angry tone.

"I just took you to Hawaii. We haven't even been flying for an hour and now you want me to take you on another vacation?"

That was not what I heard his wife say nor could it have possibly been interpreted that way. However, that was the message received by her husband and he responded defensively—and aggressively—for no reason at all. For some reason, he interpreted her comment to mean that he was expected to go on another vacation, when all she did was share a photo of a resort highlighted in the magazine.

This is how the relational space between a couple can become polluted. Once this occurs, the woman responds defensively, which only causes her partner to become reactive to her response, and once that happens the space between them becomes uncomfortable. Each of them react to the discomfort, until the space becomes dangerous. Both then respond to the danger in the space they co-created and are struggling to occupy. This often results in a heated conflict or some level of disconnecting. The problem is, if we don't know about the space and how to take responsibility for it, we will unwittingly pollute it.

Hedy Schleifer, MA, LHMC, an internationally-known couples therapist and relationship coach, teaches in her workshops about the three invisible connectors: *the relational space, crossing the bridge,* and *the encounter.* Having studied with Hedy and completed her three-year Master Class, I have learned and applied her techniques to re-connect couples by cleaning the relational space they occupy together. It is not a difficult process, but it requires a big fat "yes" from each of the partners in order to be successful. Both must be willing to learn the process.

The Art of Being Present

Here is an introduction to the three invisible connecters.

The Jewish philosopher, Martin Buber, said that each partner does not make up the relationship. It does not live in one or the other. It lives in the space between each other. He called this the "sacred space." It is also the playground for our children. Our pets live in that space, too, and like the children, they are affected by any pollution in the space. The children feel the climate of the space, which all too often can leave emotional scars as they grow. We've seen how pets naturally hide under the bed if the space remains polluted. Luckily, they can remove themselves from the tension.

The children can't. They somehow feel responsible and even guilty that they are not able to fix whatever is causing the polluted space.

In order for couples to create and maintain a conscious relationship, they must know about the space and take responsibility to maintain its sacred nature. Schleifer says that when we don't know about the space we unconsciously pollute it with a word, a look, a judgment, a criticism, a reaction, or a dialogue. In order to understand our partners, as well as to appreciate and negotiate our differences, she says that we must learn about their neighborhood, meaning the world in which they personally live.

This takes curiosity!

This takes paying attention!

This takes being present!

Each partner lives in a different world, based upon their history and experiences. It is the responsibility of each to learn the language of the other as well as their perceptions, their wounds and their stories. Couples often live together for years without really knowing the essence of their partner. They may end up living lives of quiet desperation or a not-so-quiet desperation. Either way, they live in a dis-connected state.

When they met, each had been wearing their survival suits, the ones created early in their childhood for adaptation and protection. John Bradshaw refers to the survival suit as the "false self" or the "adaptive self." When two parties in a relationship are struggling, their authentic selves become tucked deeply within their facade, afraid to be exposed. The longer they stay in hiding, for fear of punishment or shame, the larger the survival suit becomes. To really know our partners, they must uncover their survival suit, which is not easy!

Our survival suit protected us when we were young and vulnerable. During our youth, we needed to adapt in order to survive the dysfunction in our families of origin. That's because every family is dysfunctional, to a greater or lesser degree. Conscious parenting was not something that was brought to our attention when many of us grew up. Parents often parented as they had been parented, which in todays' climate, can be troublesome.

Doing what comes naturally, then, was not always healthy. As we grew older, the suit was no longer useful. It actually became counter-productive. After wearing it for so many years, we became accustomed to it, believing that the suit is really who we were.

It is not who we really are.

Who we really are lies beneath the façade, which for some becomes rigid armor. We are not the suit. Our authentic self, our essence, lies within, and each person in a relationship must be present enough to pay attention to that and be curious enough to find out what is underneath. Only then can a relationship become truly interesting and thrive.

So what do we do? Before we can listen with a fully present being we need to learn how to actually be present. This is not as easy as it sounds because most of us are not used to being in this state of mind. There are too many distractions in our lives, always ready to interfere with staying present. Technology has transformed our lives, and not always in a good way. Phones ring, texts chime, messages ding, emails pile up, clients are demanding, children need attention, family and friends require the same, and exhaustion ensues. As a result, we have limited time and energy to take care of the space in our relationships, which is our most precious tenure. For many of us, our relationships are neglected until it's often too late. Is it any wonder why more than 50 percent of marriages in this country end in divorce?

Relationships matter!

So what is the art of being present? In order to be fully present for your partner, you must make time. Not just time, but time without any distractions; otherwise it won't work. There is only so much time available to us in our everyday lives. Our partners and children know if they are valued by the quality of time we spend with them. This is also true of our aging parents that we too often neglect.

We make time to have our hair cut, watch a movie, see sporting events, or listen to news reports. We carve out the time to attend a concert, tend to our garden, work out at the gym, or hang out with friends and family, but we don't set aside time to just be with our partner to learn about their day and, most important, to work out a conflict before it becomes a war. When this attention is lacking, nothing can get resolved. When conflicts are swept under the carpet the space grows more contaminated and the carpet can begin to look like the Swiss Alps—way too steep to climb. We either explode or withdraw, depending upon each of our styles in dealing with stress and meanwhile the chasm grows wider and morphs into an even bigger disconnect.

In that case, says Schleifer, a conflict can become an opportunity!

What does she mean? It's an opportunity for growth, change, and raising the level of intimacy. Conflict, when handled with care, can drain the relational swamp, clear the air and cleanse the polluted space, but only if we know how to do it, apply it and integrate it into our daily lives, just as one brushes their teeth and showers.

This is when our survival suit disappears and our essence emerges. Here's how it works:

A couple sits in two chairs, facing one another, leaning slightly forward, about 18 inches apart (45 centimeters for metric system lovers), with both feet on the floor. Why 18 inches? In neuro-biology, that is the distance needed for presencing. Think about holding a baby in your arms. There is approximately 18 inches between the baby and you. That's the kind of intimate space, which is needed to make this work.

I then instruct the woman to place her legs inside her partners and to just breathe. I encourage both of them to focus on their partner with warm eyes and an open heart. After all, the assumption is they both showed up and hired me to be their change agent so resistance is not exactly welcome.

"Look into the eyes of your partner," I tell them. "Be grateful that you are alive. Feel your aliveness as you continue to breathe and see who showed up!

I point from one to the other.

"Look who's here with you!"

This is when I give them a moment to "see" each other.

"Notice the landscape of your partner's face, and without saying a word, thank your partner for being here. Place your palms together, holding hands slightly apart on your laps, and breathe deeply again. Take a few moments to feel the skin of your partner in a touch only the two of you know so well. Remember, the skin is the largest organ in our body. Feel the inside of the palm of your partner, and touch their fingers and take another deep breath. Allow yourself to see the child in your partner's eyes. Imagine how they might have looked as a child. Stay focused on each other's eyes, which are the true windows of the soul. Stay still and silent and breathe again."

All the while, I keep shifting my index finger back and forth from one pair of eyes to the other, as a reminder to stay focused.

This dual meditation should take about five minutes and it should feel like a dance. That is the art of presencing, of being present with your partner. I'm sure that couples who want to reconnect can afford five minutes a day to nourish their relationship. What about you?

In his book, *The Road Less Traveled*, M. Scott Peck defines love as "the willingness to extend yourself to nurture another person's spiritual growth as well as your own." I have never known a better definition. Words are not important when two partners remain present. What we know from neuro-biology is that the brain is the only organ in the body that cannot self-regulate. It needs another brain. When two brains resonate together, the central nervous system calms down. This creates a *brain bridge*.

Barbra Streisand's song, People Who Need People, says it all. It does not imply codependency at all. Instead, it literally means that in order for people to stay connected they need each other. Our brains crave connection and attachment. It fills the heart with a sense of belonging and it makes a person feel that they matter. It confirms our existence in this world! Isn't that what each of us need? Isn't that what couples want and need in a relationship?

We all want to feel as if we belong—to those we love and to the world. We want to feel loved and lovable—and to experience a secure attachment to another human being, something we may never have experienced throughout our entire life. A lack of these human needs creates chaos, low self-esteem, and a collage of negative feelings about oneself and others, which all too often results in depression and a feeling of alienation. Eventually, this makes its way into the cells of our body and affects our immune system in potentially damaging ways. It can also disturb the synchronicity of our mind-body connection, leaving us emotionally starved and full of relentless stress, which can often cause disease.

Presencing is not a difficult process to learn if you want to enrich and restore the love you once had, or the love you wish to maintain. That's because love is like a living organism. It needs to be fed and nurtured, protected and secured. It requires attention, not unlike a plant that needs sunlight, water, fertilizer and the correct environment. Given what it needs, a plant will flourish. Many of us as children did not have our needs met. We lacked proper nourishment, even if our plates were full at dinnertime. Consequently, we keep searching for this kind of love in our partners, often repeating the past and eventually giving up, thinking we picked the wrong partner, when in fact, we are just trying to get it right.

When your partner receives what he or she needs, the relationship will benefit and thrive. It's as simple as that. It takes time, commitment and money. It is worth the investment in your relationship and your life.

Celebrating the Experts

Harville Hendrix, the founder of Imago Relationship Therapy (IRT) and author of *Getting the Love You Want*, created a style of couple's therapy that focuses on relational counseling, which transforms a conflict into an opportunity to grow and heal. Shleifer adapted her work to create the potential for the same outcome. Each of them contributed to helping couples re-connect.

There have been endless contributions made in the field of couple counseling. New and improved techniques are emerging all the time. There is no one way or best way. This is determined by what works best for each therapist and what clicks with the couples. Many therapists, like myself, incorporate several modalities to apply as needed. It's like golf. If you only have one club in your golf bag, chances are you will play a less than satisfying game of golf. When techniques are synthesized to produce a desired outcome, it often generates a new technology. Many therapists, including me, have stacked, compiled, modified and included many of the modalities that have been used by wizard-like therapists, as well as adding our own original insights and ideas.

I have employed the techniques of several, some of whom I've already mentioned, including the works of John Bradshaw, *The New York Times* best-selling author and creator of *Maintaining Healthy Relationships*, which uses his Fair Fighting Rules, Inner Child Work, and work within the recovering community, as well as how to employ the Change model for more effective communication. I have studied with Lori and Morris Gordon who developed PAIRS, (Practical Applications of Intimate Relationship Skills). I have utilized the works of NLP (Neuro-Linguistics Programming), and had the privilege of studying with Richard Bandler and John Grinder, who deliberated in detail the works of Virginia Satir (Family Therapy) and Milton Erickson, MD, (hypnosis), with the purpose of using teachings from those that do it best in the fields of sales, education and therapy. I attended workshops and listened to the tapes of Tony Robbins, and viewed recordings of Esther Perel and John Gottman, who introduced the concept of The Four Horsemen of the Apocalypse, a metaphor that describes the four main behaviors that will cause decimation of a relationship. I am certified as a Master technician in EMDR, (eye movement desensitization and reprocessing) having had the honor of studying with Francine Shapiro, who discovered this amazing technology to resolve PTSD, (Post-Traumatic

Stress Disorder). PSTD plays an important role in relationships, as we have seen all too often when one person (or both) unconsciously bring their past into the present, disrupting and polluting the relational space, as well as causing chaos and doom. The list goes on, but only serves to point out that this has been my life's work. However, it is important to note that any technique only works as well as the person using it.

Most important is giving the couple the feeling that they matter, because they do!

The Challenge of Letting Go

In the beginning, learning how to be present feels contrived and staged as do all new acquired behaviors. Learning to play the piano begins with practicing scales. Driving a car requires earning a license that can only be accomplished after instruction and practice. Learning a sport demands tedious practice, as does voice training and anything worth learning. It does not come naturally, even if an instinctive talent is present. Learning any new performance or activity needs instruction, preparation and cultivation.

The art of presencing also needs to be learned. It is something we do naturally as children, when we live in a world of wonder and curiosity. It is only when we grow into adulthood and our survival suit is glued on to our bodies that we forget what we once knew so well. Beginning again is like learning how to play an instrument correctly after stumbling through it on our own. Once accomplished, the results are well worth the effort and extremely gratifying.

Once we know how to be present to our partners, the three invisible connectors can be introduced. However, they cannot be successful without presencing. It is our entry way into the first invisible connector, the relational space which opens the door to crossing the bridge, and finally approaching the encounter.

Now that I have covered the art of presencing, let's move forward to the relational space where a couple lives—the space between the two people, just as children share relational space on a playground and the same space where pets feel at home. This space automatically becomes contaminated if a couple does not know how to take care of it. Presencing is the starting point of making any space clean. When couples look into the warm eyes of each other and sense an open heart, something magical can happen. The central nervous system relaxes. Tension in the body is reduced. Shoulders that might be tight go soft. Blood pressure drops. Tears may well up. This may be the first time that two people have looked deeply and lovingly into each other's eyes.

"Oh! It's you!" Schleifer often bellows, demonstrating the start of presencing.

Couples usually smile. I ask them to thank the other for coming—for showing up, for being present. The space is now fertile for crossing the bridge. I give specific instructions on how to do this. One partner assumes the role of the host while the other is the visitor. Each chooses the role. Each may want the other to be the host or the visitor, but it is essential that each person choose their own role. Sometimes, this produces a conflict.

"Choose the role that would best benefit the relationship," I say, in those cases.

There is usually a pregnant pause before one party responds.

"Okay, I'll be the host or visitor," says one, leaving the other to be satisfied with the opposite role.

Most couples feel awkward starting the process. They don't know how to be present or what to say, so it is necessary that I coach them and teach them to let go.

Anne and David

This couple came into my office perplexed, anxious and deeply hurt. They had been carrying a gunny sack of anger and emotional pain for many years. Divorce seemed to be their next step. A relative had told them about ECCT (Encounter-Centered Couples Therapy) and referred them to me for counseling. Reluctantly, Anne made the appointment and both showed up early on a Monday morning. Anne immediately spoke.

"This is our last resort. We are tired of fighting, tired of each other and have no more resources to use. We have both been in therapy, individually and as a couple. Nothing seemed to work. Our decision was to separate and then file for divorce. David's sister insisted that we make an appointment with you. he said we could always get a divorce. Give it this last chance, so here we are."

David shrugged his shoulders and nervously responded.

"Yep. That's right. Too much time, too much pain and not enough to rebuild. I was not looking forward to this visit, but we both decided not to throw in the towel yet. I guess we both want it to work but are exhausted trying with no results. My sister had seen you with her husband a few years back and said you saved their marriage. They told us they still use the tools you taught them and feel grateful to you for the work you did with them. "

"Quite honestly, I did not save their marriage. They did. I gave them the resources they needed and instilled hope. They took the tools home and practiced. They made it a priority or it would not have been successful."

The pain I could see with Anne and David was palpable. But beneath the obvious current of despair was a glimmer of hope. That is how our session began. After acquiring some history, I learned that they had been married 18 years, had two children, a son, Timothy, 15, and a daughter, Belinda, who had just turned 13. I asked if they had any pets. They shared that Daisy, a Cocker Spaniel rescue, had been with them nearly eight years.

"Do you have a photo of your children and Daisy?"

They were both quick to respond. David reached in his pocket and drew out his wallet, containing photos of each of the children, and Daisy. Anne took her phone out with photos of the family taken just days before. Daisy was sitting in the front row.

I smiled.

"You are very lucky. You have a beautiful family."

They both agreed, Anne began welling up with tears.

"Yes, we do," she said. "That's one reason we're here."

There was a moment of silence for them to reflect on what Anne had said. I asked them to demonstrate how they worked on a conflict.

"Take any issue that becomes an argument and show me how it sounds and looks."

I sat adjacent to them as they squirmed a bit, on the sofa, bewildered at how to respond.

"I am not sure what you mean," David said.

"Just show me how you discuss a conflict."

"You mean choose something we fight about?"

"Exactly. Choose an issue and pretend I'm a fly on the wall and let me see how you communicate. You have 13 minutes to create this scenario so I can observe you. At the end of the 13 minutes, I will call 'STOP' and you will do so even if you are in the middle of a sentence."

They looked confused. They each wanted me to know that this was something neither of them were ever asked to do in any of their previous therapy sessions. I told them I understood, but that there was a method to this madness and to just be patient. They chose a common conflict. He chose how she mis-manages money. It could have been any topic. I was interested in looking at their means of communication, just as a physician examines an x-ray.

It didn't take more than a minute before their emotions flared up, carrying their voices to a higher pitch, which quickly morphed into a vitriolic shouting match. Their body language reflected their tone and dialectical exchange. Their animation shifted in many directions. Arms waved, legs shook, and bodies shifted, either moving toward or away from each other. Their skin tone changed from pale to blush, deepening in shades as they continued to shout at one another. Annie and David seemed unaware that I was in the room. Their dialogue took on a life of its own.

At precisely 13 minutes I brought my arm down and shouted, "STOP." They looked at each other, then turned their faces to me. Anne took a deep breath.

"Whew. I'm exhausted."

David nodded.

"Me too. We do this too often and it leads to nowhere except frustration and futility. I can't keep this up. My blood pressure rises and I need a drink to calm me down. It doesn't work."

"I imagine this is your style of working on a conflict," I said. "Right?"

"Yep! This is us in action. Why 13 minutes?"

"That's all the time needed to observe the process. Imagine if someone was in your home and heard you as you were and suddenly shouted, 'stop' at a moment when things were becoming out of control. Everyone present, including Daisy, would have been greatly relieved."

This is when the teaching could begin.

"You were the Wigerian couple."

Perplexed, the both looked at me like I was speaking another language. This is the title that had been given to my colleagues and me who had attended a Master Class presented by Schleifer when we began our training in Encounter-Centered Couples Therapy. The Wigerian couple is a fictitious word that metaphorically means the couple that comes from another planet. They only speak Wigerian.

"I want you to imagine you were just in a diner and saw another couple sitting across from you. That couple represents who you were a few minutes ago. You were able to see them, but because they were from Wigeria, you could not understand a word they spoke. Tell me your observations, based solely on what your saw. Remember that you could not understand them, as they spoke a language you had never heard. Describe what you noticed and interpreted, and then tell me why."

This was not easy for either of them. They had difficulty keeping what they heard, rather than what they saw, out of the content. I had to pause a few times until they finally understood.

"She was very distraught" said Anne.

"Give me evidence without any words she might have said."

"Well, she raised her voice. Her demeanor changed rapidly. She went from calm to anger in a matter of moments after her partner attacked her."

"How do you know he attacked her?"

"That was easy. He began insulting her."

"How do you know they were insulting words, Annie? Remember, you don't know their language."

"Well, she appeared angry after he spoke. I imagined he might have said something she didn't like.

"Of course he did," said David.

"How do you know?' I said. "You also don't understand the language."

"Because that's exactly what I did just before Annie blew up."

This went on for about 20 minutes. The purpose was to objectify their behavior so they could see how they looked if they were observing themselves, which most couples can't do. When the process was complete and they were able to understand the value of the exercise, they could see themselves in a mirror and begin to become aware of how this behavior had impacted their own relationship.

"Oh my God!" both said simultaneously.

"Oh my God is right! Imagine how this might affect your kids and Daisy if they are chronically subjected to this behavior. Imagine how this destroys love, affection, sex and the relationship."

I said this without judgment or criticism, as it's basically a scientific fact of what can happen when two adults poison a home for its other inhabitants.

"This is what John Gottman refers to as The Four Horsemen of the Apocalypse—contempt, criticism, judgment and stonewalling. They destroy relationships."

The ensuing silence spoke louder than words. Annie and David looked at one another with sorrow and shame. They actually described their space as sad, scary, shameful, pathetic and sick, before adding the word insightful. I repeated each word after it had been spoken. Those were the words they reflected back to me when I asked them to describe the space between them after the work was done.

Now they were ready to learn the art of presencing. I moved the two chairs across from the sofa where they were seated to face each other and invited them to sit. The teaching and instruction of presencing was done and they sat quietly, reflecting silently on their shared experience. I told them what to do and how to do it, and they followed my instructions to the letter. Tears flowed from both their eyes as I stayed with them, reminding them to stay connected through locking their eyes on each other. No words were spoken and no questions were asked. I could hear their sniffles, sobs and breathing as I facilitated this dynamic process of transformation. I felt privileged and blessed to be their change agent. I knew in that moment that this couple were going to get through this co-created prison of sorts. As they sat in the eye of this beautiful storm, I felt so lucky to be their benign witness.

What Do We Do Now?

The art of being present is not only the preparation for crossing the bridge and embracing what needs to be encountered. It is also a gateway to learning how to listen with a third ear. The "third ear" is a concept introduced by psychoanalyst Theodor Reik, and it refers to the practice of listening for the deeper layers of meaning in order to glean what has not been said outright. It means perceiving the emotional underpinnings conveyed when someone is speaking to you. Most important, it teaches us how to be conscious, patient and attentive to another person, something that is lacking in most relationships. This type of active listening is the key to insuring respect for each other and offers anyone hope to being capable of repairing or reigniting the love that is the foundation of all relationships.

*Out of suffering have emerged
the strongest souls; the most massive
characters are seared with scars.*

—**Kahlil Gibran**

6

Please Don't Judge, Criticize, Blame, Stonewall, or Avoid Me

In the previous chapter, I described the importance of the art of presencing. If your partner doesn't understand the value of being present, or does not care enough to learn how, any conflict between the two of you will never be resolved.

Being present means staying focused and mindful of the other person. This is accomplished by looking into the eyes of your partner and staying conscious in the here and now. You may know this as "living in the moment."

This the precursor to *crossing the bridge*, the next invisible connector.

In *The Kaminsky Method*, a television series on Netflix, Michael Douglas plays the owner and acting coach of his school, aptly named THE KAMINSKY METHOD. In one episode, he teaches the art of *mirroring*, an elementary acting exercise for beginners.

Mirroring might as well be called presencing, as its goal is to teach students how to stay present, fully engaged and in the moment with their partner. The goal is identical in presencing. Douglas has his students mirror or replicate exactly what their partner is doing, as if there were a mirror between them. If their partner's hand creates a circle, their hand follows along, emulating the exact behavior.

This is precisely what is done in crossing the bridge.

With so many distractions in the course of the day, this is not easy to do, but it's necessary to achieve effective communication. Once presencing is—and I say *learned* because being present does not come naturally—a couple can move forward to conscious, active listening, understanding and resolution. In most families, our role models are our parents, who did not always exemplify this essential trait in communication. Therefore, in our own defense, how were we to know how to be present? We only know what we know!

The Curse of the Pot Roast

My mother was not the best cook. It wasn't her fault, as she learned how to cook from her mother, my grandmother. Grandma Eva came from Poland to America at the turn of the 20th century to join my grandfather, Moishe, who fled Warsaw to escape the persecution of Jews and serving in the military. Like most immigrants, Eva arrived with little, but she managed to bring a small tin pan that her mother had given her before she left Poland, along with a few other salient items. That tin pan was about 12 inches square. My grandmother used it to cook everything she had learned from her mother. Being impoverished, not unlike Golda and Tevya from *Fiddler on the Roof*, they cooked with bare essentials, including inexpensive cuts of kosher meat, and condiments were always scarce.

I never knew about Heinz ketchup until I was in my twenties. My mother went to the Thrifty Market in South Beach, where many poor, first generation Jews migrated and bought only non-brand items. She, like her mother, was a champion shopper. My father used to say that she could take a dollar and turn it into four. He also said I could take four dollars and turn it into one! That pan was a household item until my mother gave it to me when I married. I kept it, primarily for sentimental reasons until I was nearly 50 years old.

My mother used that pan to make pot roast, otherwise known as brisket. I hated it. We had it every Thursday, so when I got off the bus from school and neared our apartment, I could already smell the unsavory, odious flavor of our inevitable dinner.

"Shit, it's Thursday. Pot roast."

My mother went to the kosher butcher and bought the cheapest piece of meat, which was known as bruschtekle. It was tough, first because it was kosher and not aged, and secondly because it was the cheapest cut of meat from the bottom of the cow's belly. No one knew its origin. They only knew that it was affordable. No one in my family has ever been to a restaurant and ordered pot roast or tasted anyone else's pot roast, so they had no frame of reference to judge their own cooking, and for them, it was tasty.

My mother took the meat, laid it fat-side-up in the tin pan, and folded over the ends because the pan was too small. She added a potato, an onion, a couple carrots, salt, pepper and a bottle of Thrifty Maid ketchup. Somehow, we swallowed it, probably out of obligation.

"Why don't you get a bigger pan?" I always asked her.

"It makes juice when you fold it over!"

In Yiddish, this response is referred to as a *Bubba Miseh*—an old wives' tale—which some of us simply call bullshit.

But I accepted her explanation. It made sense to me as a teenager and that was how I learned to make pot roast. When I became a young bride, I acquired a cookbook that had been created by a group of women in my neighborhood, all of whom were members of a local affiliate of a national cancer organization. We all shared recipes from our personal history. This is how I learned how to make brisket. For some reason, pot roast was not included in our makeshift cookbook and I wasn't about to offer my mother's version. However, I used my mother's tin pan that she gave me when I married, so the meat had its original home for roasting. Unlike my mother, though, I followed the brisket recipe that turned out to be my children's favorite meal, even until today.

While married to my last husband, Mike, a meat fabricator and proprietor of a gourmet grocery business in Miami Beach, similar to Dean & Deluca in New York City, he asked if I could make pot roast.

"Pot roast! You like pot roast?"

"Yes, pot roast. I love pot roast!"

I recalled making a face, screwing up my eyes and wondering how anyone could like pot roast. Just the sound of those two words triggered my olfactory senses and resurrected the abhorrent smell that had been dormant in my brain for quite some time.

"Why don't you just bring it home from the hot counter in the store? Or better yet, just bring it home from the freezer and I will heat it up."

The recipe had been prepared on the hot counter inside the store or could be purchased as a frozen item to be used whenever the customer preferred.

Mike looked at me, shaking his head.

"No!" he said. "I would prefer you make it at home."

It is important to note that his mother was an amazing cook. In fact, it was she who founded the grocery store in the 1940s, preparing recipes she had created and brought with her from back home in Lithuania. I didn't know what to say, as I realized I had no excuse that would be acceptable, so I capitulated to his wishes and went to a kosher butcher, a place I had never visited in my adult life.

"May I have a piece of bruschtekle, please?".

"Bruschtekle! What are you going to use it for?"

The butcher sounded strangely curious.

"Pot roast."

"That's not the best piece of meat for a nice pot roast. It's used mainly for soup flavoring."

I appreciated his advice but chose the cut of meat that my mother always used, never considering that he might know better than my mother. When it came to cooking, I was still in the same trance that I had been in since birth.

I went home, took out the meat, and laid it exactly in the pan as my mother had always done. I folded the ends over, adding the same ingredients she had always used, except I used a different brand of ketchup. I chose Heinz, an upgrade in my mind, along with a bit of garlic, which was my own touch. It wasn't long before I heard Mike open the door to our apartment.

"What stinks?"

I thought it was strange that he had the same response as I had when I was a teenager, coming home on Thursdays to the same putrid smell.

"It's the pot roast you asked me to make. It will be ready in a few minutes."

Mike opened the oven.

"Joni, the pot's too small. Look—the meat doesn't even fit in the pan."

"This is the pan my mother always used. You have to fold the meat over inside it to make the gravy."

It should come as no surprise that our dinner was tossed into the garbage. Mike asked me to never buy that cut of meat again. He was happy to share his mother's recipe, which did not include ko-sher meat, which was, by the way, also not aged or tenderized. I was greatly relieved, as I knew her recipe was a hard act to follow. The following day, he brought home the pot roast from the hot counter as when he served it the smell was nothing like what I remembered. Dinner was delicious, and I loved it!

Who Knew?

It's not that I didn't have a dozen or more cook books on my kitch-en shelf. It's not that I couldn't Google a recipe on my own. I just did what came naturally. I made the pot roast as I had learned it from my mother, the same way I learned how to communicate. My parents never resolved anything. Their differences were settled with either my mother capitulating to my father or my father having a personal protest and giving everyone in the household the "silent violence," which meant he stonewalled all of us. Most of the time, any conflict was swept under the carpet until the carpet began to resemble the terrain of the Swiss Alps. After a few days passed, all was forgotten until the next blow up.

This story of the stinky pot roast shows how we only know what we know. We inherit what we were exposed to as children and repeat it in our adult relationships, believing that this is the way it's supposed to be!

When we don't know how to be present it becomes a mulita-generational tradition, like the pan my grandmother gave my mother, which my mother handed down to me. We assume that is the way it should happen. It becomes a legacy learned from our family of origin. Even though we may think so at first, doing what comes naturally doesn't necessarily mean that it's right, healthy or makes sense.

The analogy of my mother's pot roast generalizes how we carry forth family systems and traditions when we marry and create families of our own. Many of our behaviors, thoughts, beliefs, and values come from how we were raised and how our parents were raised. These patterns go back generations and it's only when they don't work with our new partners that any conflict begins.

As Schleifer says with great enthusiasm, "Conflict is a friend. What an opportunity!"

A Model for Change

Couples can only grow when they are able to resolve conflict, which ultimately raises their levels of intimacy. But this can only happen with the art of presencing!

In his work with couples, John Gottman describes what he refers to as The Four Horsemen of the Apocalypse: criticism, contempt, defensiveness and stonewalling. In the New Testament, The Four Horsemen of the Apocalypse is a metaphor depicting the end of times, which Gottman borrows to depict the demise of a relationship. These four behaviors will surely destroy any relationship if they become a chronic characteristic of a couple's communication style.

In *The Change Model*, John Bradshaw states that criticism can be replaced with a complaint or a concern, as did Lori and Morris Gordon, the founders of PAIRS (Practical Applications of Intimate Relationship Skills).

"You" messages are replaced with "I" messages. "I" messages are self-responsible statements representing what one sees or hears—how one feels—to go along with how one interprets and what one needs. After expressing these concerns, a contract is made.

Individual parts of the model include perception (what is seen or heard), feelings, thoughts (what is interpreted), and what a person needs. Finally, after genuine communication, a verbal contract secures an agreement.

For example, consider the following dialogue:

"When I *saw* you spending so much time with Mary at the party last night, I *felt* hurt and upset. I *imagined* that you were flirting with her, and I *needed* your attention to be on me. Can we *agree* that the next time we are in a mixed social situation, you are conscious of spending less time with other women and more time with me?"

This recipe for open communication essentially eliminates the word "you" and reduces the instinct for being defensive and the probability of an argument. Challenging your partner with the word "you" instead of "I" is an invitation for a fight. Your partner will become defensive, ready to argue that it was not the case. The space immediately becomes dangerous and you both alternatively react to the danger in the space.

According to Schleifer, in a situation like this, two types of people begin to behave accordingly. *Hailstormers* become more aggressive, usually raising their voices, while *turtles* become withdrawn and shut down. Neither party feels honored or heard and the fighting escalates from there. Make no mistake. Hailstormers and turtles can be of either gender. Men and women don't have exclusive rights to these behaviors.

In addition to refraining from using the *you* word, such as, "*You* are always late. I know you will *never* be on time," avoid using words like *always, never, should* and *must*. They express a demand, and are not helpful when having a dialogue.

Crossing the Bridge

Let's examine the second invisible connector, which eliminates any criticism, defensiveness, contempt or stonewalling. In a process called *crossing the bridge*, there is no dialogue between partners—only a visit and an encounter. It creates all the elements needed for a healthy, conscious relationship by providing a platform for each partner to consider and understand their partner's perceptions, feelings, interpretations, needs and wishes. Its economy of words, reflective listening, eye contact and positive intention creates a wavelength for growth, which deepens and intensifies the relational space between partners.

What was formerly polluted becomes clean. What was previously fueling friction and upheaval morphs into understanding and empathy. Once this technique is learned and practiced, conflict becomes an opportunity for growth, closeness and connection.

So how does it work? Let's observe a couple who came to me for help.

Anne and David

Remember these two from the previous chapter? A week later, Anne and David arrived at my office for their follow-up appointment. They brought in a framed professional photograph of their children and placed it on a table in front of them. I had placed fresh flowers there to create a warm and inviting atmosphere. I already had two chairs in position, facing each other. Anne and David took the cue and sat in the chairs without any instruction from me. They told me that the week since our meeting had been better, which I was delighted to hear. I congratulated them once more for making the effort to try again.

"That was a remarkable exercise you had us do," said Anne. "I didn't realize how emotionally drained I was just from watching us in the diner."

David agreed. They were able to reflect on their behavior as they recognized their emotional fatigue and failure to solve their issue. By objectifying themselves in the diner, they clearly saw how their communication style was damaging and futile. They were also reminded about how their behavior affects their children.

"So once again ... do I have a big fat 'yes' from both of you?" I said.

They looked at each other, then glanced back to me. Anne nodded, followed by a nod and a shoulder shrug from David.

"That is not terribly big or fat. I need to be certain of your intention. Let's try it again. Do I have a big fat 'yes' from both of you?"

Both responded simultaneously, as if I had given them a command.

"Yes!"

They looked at each other once more and then turned their attention to me. I told them that without a strong commitment we would not be successful.

"Let's get started. Position yourselves as I had instructed you last week."

Anne and David sat 18 inches apart, eyeball to eyeball. They leaned forward, placed their hands in each other's and looked into each other's eyes. The emotional fatigue that was so apparent last week, was gone and they appeared eager to begin.

"Lean forward and connect so that your eyes never leave each other. Place your hands together and feel the familiar touch of each other. Thank your partner for showing up, but just with your eyes! Now, still without words, share your hopes, wishes and dreams with each other. Look deeply into your partner's eyes and let them know how grateful you are to be alive and for all the things you share together. You can do this with your eyes. Words are not necessary." Since my chair was in the middle, apart about a foot from theirs, I continued moving my finger slowly back and forth between their eyes as a reminder to stay connected to each other.

"This is how you discover the landscape in your partner's face. When we begin crossing the bridge, you will learn a new language, as well. Just stay with each other."

When I asked them in a soft voice to see the child in the other, as if their partner were seven years old, tears welled up in both their eyes.

"Stay together. Just keep looking, with an open heart and soft eyes. You can do this. Just stay focused and remain connected."

The process lasted about five or six minutes. The next step was to ask Anne and David to share how the space felt between them after they did the presencing. They were aware of the shift in the space and responded with words that seemed to surprise them.

"It feels warm," Anne said.

"Safe," said David.

I asked them to toss out words that described the space. This part of the process was slow to unfold. I repeated each word they shared. By reflecting back on the words they had just spoken, Anne and David were able to learn what active listening is all about.

We moved next into the *three wildest dreams*.

I had them write down three dreams they wanted to actualize in their lifetime. The dreams were called *wild* so they could imagine whatever they wanted to put on their respective horizon, without boundaries. When I asked them to share their dreams, they were surprised to learn that they were identical. As Anne and David read aloud I wrote down all three dreams they had shared. I read it back to them so they could hear their dreams spoken, which became another reflective listening lesson unwittingly planted into their sub-conscious brains.

Anne and David were now ready to cross the bridge to the world of the other.

I gave them explicit instructions, first to prepare them for the *visit* and the *encounter*, which make up the third invisible connector. I asked them to leave behind all of their perceptions, stories, prejudices, emotions, beliefs, preconceived notions, and behaviors. All of those had to stay back on their side of the bridge. The only item they could take with them was a plastic bag with a passport and visa. It had to be plastic so they could see it was empty, except for those items. Everything else had to be left on their side of the bridge. Otherwise, it would be considered "an illegal import." I would act as a customs officer to ensure that their "stuff" would remain in their own world and not be illegally transported to the world of their partner.

Next, Anne and David had to choose who was going to be the visitor and who would be the host. They were both reluctant to make a choice, but after some intrapersonal consideration, Anne chose to be the host and David was content to be the visitor.

I took my time to coach them through this process, explaining their respective roles in detail. They understood the concept, but both acknowledged their anxiety. David's leg shook rapidly. Anne sat quietly, holding back tears. I decided to slow the process down by doing a breathing meditation to help them relax. As they began focusing on their breath, I noticed David's leg stopped shaking and Anne released her tears.

"I'm scared," Anne said. "What if I can't do this? What if I get it wrong?"

"There's no right or wrong," I said. "Everything that will happen has a positive intention. We'll go slowly and I will help you every step of the way."

Once they understood the rules and goals, we began. I pulled my chair closer and leaned over so I could assist them gently as we moved into the ritual.

"Anne, as the host, you are going to invite David to cross the bridge and come over to your neighborhood. Then you are going to take him down a street called . . . whatever name you want to give it, anything you want to share with David. For example, it can be called the street of misunderstanding, the street of fear, anxiety, loneliness, or worry—whatever you want to name it. So it will sound like this: 'David, I would like to invite you to my neighborhood, down my street called fill in the blank.' Do you understand?"

Anne nodded and waited for me to continue. I kept reminding them to look into each other's eyes and stay connected through every beat of the process.

"It's not easy to stay present, but it's absolutely necessary. This encounter is a meeting of your human essences, your two souls and your two life forces. It provides an opportunity for you to drop your survival suits, the protective armor you may not even realize you've been wearing for so long, so that your authentic selves can emerge—perhaps for the first time. From now on, you are not going to need them because they do not serve any positive purpose. You will soon discover that beneath the suits you have been wearing for so long is the real you."

I spoke softly to David, giving him instructions on his role as the visitor.

"After Anne invites you to visit her neighborhood and the street she has chosen and named, you will respond as if you have been invited to visit someone's home. You'll say, 'Thank you, Anne, for the invitation,' and then repeat what she requested, with something like, 'I am happy to cross the bridge to your neighborhood and visit the street called fill in the blank.'"

I told them there was an imaginary bridge between their neighborhoods. In neurobiology, this bridge is called the *brain bridge*. Our brain is the only organ in the body that cannot self-regulate. It can only do that through the resonance of another brain, when new neuro-pathways are created with the capacity to become more relationally intelligent. The brain's plasticity makes it capable of changing old habits and creating new ones, in the service of oneself as well as the relationship.

When you hear someone say, "This is who I am. I have always been like this. I cannot change. Just accept me as I am," you should know that it is not true. We *can* change, because of the flexible plasticity in our brains. We only have to choose to make the changes and learn how to manifest them. We can grow further if and when we choose to do so. This teaching reflects information well-known to psychologists, psychiatrists and other mental health professionals.

David was instructed to slowly walk across the imaginary bridge and arrive in Anne's neighborhood. Once there, he would announce his presence. Anne would thank him for coming and the encounter would begin. After prepping each regarding their roles, I instructed the host to speak with as few words as possible, using not more than five or six.

Anne paused for a long time.

"I don't know what to say."

"Say the name of your street for starters."

Anne hesitated and rolled her eyes upward, as if picturing what her street represented and what she wanted to call it. After a few silent moments, she said, "I want to invite you down the street of not feeling safe."

David followed my instructions perfectly.

"Anne, what I heard you say is that you want to invite me to your neighborhood to visit the street called 'not feeling safe.' Am I with you?"

I gave David a nod of approval and leaned into him once more , smiling, as I told him what his response should be: "Tell me more."

David responded. "Tell me more."

Silence.

No one moved.

Finally, Anne looked at me as if to ask me what comes next. I spoke briefly, telling her to describe her street in five words or less.

"I'm scared to express my feelings to you, "she said to David.

That was more than five words but it was specific, sensory-based information, so it was acceptable.

David looked perplexed.

"You have nothing to be afraid of," he said.

I stopped the process to explain that in this ritual of crossing the bridge there is no dialogue. David was only to repeat Anne's words and respond with one of two phrases:

"Am I with you?" and "Tell me more."

"You mean I can't respond to her?" he said. "I can't have my own thoughts as to what she says?"

He was visibly annoyed.

"Then when can I have my turn to respond?" he said.

I had to reinforce the purpose of this encounter and review the rules so that David could understand that this was not intended to be a dialogue. This took some time, but he eventually understood and we began once more.

As David began to use the allowed phrases appropriately, Anne's responses deepened. She began to feel safe and shared her feelings. David remained patient. Instead of talking over her, as he had done in the past, he listened, and the look on his face gave Anne the impression that he was hearing her as well as repeating the words she said.

There was no shouting, stonewalling, criticism, contempt, or defensiveness—just listening and repeating her words. He only rolled his eyes once— a real no-no—so I alerted him that rolling your eyes is an illegal import, which comes from his neighborhood on the other side of the bridge. I asked him to take it back from where it came. They shared some laughter, which gave levity to the process.

Making David conscious of his behavior and explaining the destructive effect it had been having on his relationship with Anne made him more mindful. He said he would try to refrain from doing it again.

"We don't expect perfection," I said, "only progress. This is not a one-time event! It's a process! It takes time, commitment and a whole lot of patience and practice. It is a new way of communicating and you'll soon see that the results are worthwhile."

Several times during this first encounter in my office, David's responses did not exactly mirror the words Anne had spoken. Whenever that occurred, I instructed Anne to say, "You got most of it. Here's what I want you to hear and understand." David tried again until Anne felt as if he was genuinely with her and that her words and needs were resonating with him. This openness and attention to detail is necessary to ensure a complete connection.

Occasionally both partners made illegal imports. Each time one slipped in, I paused the process and explained it again, until they got it. It took the entire two hours for them to cross the bridge one time. This is why I like to have a couple with me for two days because it allows the process to be fluid and unfold at a pace that suits their particular personalities and relationship.

It took Anne another half an hour and quite a few tears before she felt a sense of completion, that she had no more to say. Throughout the process, David tried hard not to respond. He sat quietly, as I had taught him, and waited for any waves of emotion to quiet down before he would once again say to Anne, "tell me more." I reminded David that she needed time to express her feelings and that he needed to give her permission to take that time. Whenever a wave of emotion surged, they allowed it to complete its energy before continuing. I reminded Anne that she had to provide the same benefit for David when it was his turn.

This was a lesson in empathy and compassion, which had both been lacking in their daily communication with each other.

During our time together, new neuro-pathways were beginning to form in their brains. Anne recognized that David *did* have the capacity to listen and David recognized that Anne *was* entitled to her feelings. Each time Anne spoke with a minimum amount of words and David repeated them, adding the phrases we had rehearsed, the give-and-take became easier. They began to integrate the process and were able to hear one another and stay present. I made sure they maintained eye contact throughout the entire process, which is a key to ensuring that the heartbeat of the exchanges are authentic and loving.

What Do We Do Now?

After the visit, I asked David to summarize what he had learned from his visit to Anne's neighborhood. As she listened to him, Anne felt genuinely heard and understood, and she appeared relieved and relaxed. Next, I had Anne and David offer each other three "appreciations," followed by sharing what was most important to them. Then I had them write down five things they had learned during the process, which they shared aloud. Finally, I asked them to describe the space, using only one word at a time. With each word expressed, I repeated it back, which served to reinforce the art and craft of effective listening.

When our time was up, I asked if they would be interested in spending two full days with me, explaining how this would be even more beneficial. They were open to the idea and said they would think about it and let me know. I told them to practice what we had done in the session, giving them a tip sheet with the steps I had taught them, including putting two chairs together, facing each other in a room, at a time when they would not be disturbed, such as when their children were asleep.

I was not surprised when Anne and David called me during the week, telling me that they had decided to commit to the two-day intensive. We were all excited to make an appointment for two weeks in advance, leaving all of us time to clear our schedules and prepare.

The next chapter will reveal what happened.

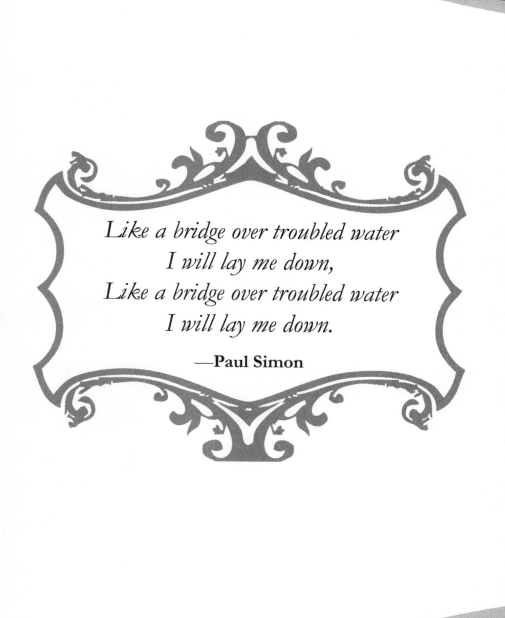

Like a bridge over troubled water
I will lay me down,
Like a bridge over troubled water
I will lay me down.

—**Paul Simon**

7

A Bridge Over Troubled Waters

As you witnessed in the previous chapter, Anne and David successfully completed their first bridge crossing. Due to the time restriction we had, I was limited in expanding the process to the next level, which would have explored the etiology of one of Anne's most telling comments. When she said that she felt "unsafe to express her feelings" I wish we could have found out more about where that came from and what continues to trigger these feelings.

Here's what we already know about human behavior: When we have a strong feeling about another person's behavior, it usually applies to the person who feels threatened in some way because of his or her history, and not because of the person who triggered their response. Anne's reaction to David—feeling unsafe to express her feelings—was triggered in the moment by his communication style, but that was not the sole reason. It's more than likely that her reaction primarily stems from an earlier childhood experience. If there had been more time, I would have asked Anne to remember a time when it didn't feel safe to verbalize her feelings.

I would have told her to grab the first memory that came to her mind because a recollection from childhood would probably have emerged, allowing me to draw a line from the feeling she was having in my office back to a childhood trauma, which caused an early wound that could certainly still be reverberating today in her relationship with David. The story she would have shared, coupled with the feelings associated with her memory, would have enlightened David and helped him to better understand Anne's history.

When this happens as part of the crossing the bridge process, empathy surfaces and a new learning pattern is revealed for both parties.

A Primer on Empathy

Empathy is the capacity to understand or feel what another person is experiencing from within their frame of reference by placing oneself in another person's position. Human beings are wired to be empathic. It's in our DNA. It's just that our own filters and history too often obfuscate our ability to be empathic so we become *re*-active instead of *pro*-active.

This might explain why David immediately became defensive when he heard Anne express her sense of feeling unsafe. In this chapter, when David and Anne return for a two-day intensive, giving us time to complete the ritual, I will demonstrate how this works when David is the host.

We know from working with individuals and couples that most of what triggers strong feelings and/or reactions usually originate with something that might have been repressed during childhood. That's just how our brain works. When we hurt early in life, we tend to inoculate ourselves against any more suffering. So when something similar occurs in the present, it fires up all the neurons in the brain, which have been dormant. Repressed feelings can suddenly surface and a wound that never healed can be ripped open once again, often without warning and in a decidedly awkward situation.

Whenever something like this occurs, empathy becomes crucial.

Anne and David Dive In

When they arrived at my office on a Friday morning, two weeks after our initial appointment, I had a positive feeling about what we were about to accomplish. They brought a photo of their children, as I had reminded them to do, and they immediately noticed another floral arrangement I had already placed on the table.

After some chatting, reviewing the past two weeks, we were ready to begin. Anne and David revealed that they had practiced the bridge crossing several times, some successfully, and others not so much. They shared their frustrations and confusion, all of which I understood, and I told them their experience was normal.

"Nobody gets this perfect, especially after only one bridge crossing. It takes time, practice, patience and perseverance. However, once you master the ritual, it becomes easier and integrated, much like brushing your teeth."

"Now it's my turn to be a host," said David, obviously eager to get started.

"Indeed, it is," I said. "Are you ready to cross the bridge?"

David and Anne sat in the same chairs I had set for them.

"Okay. Sit down and look at each other with a big open heart, with soft eyes, and a generosity of spirit."

I gave them a minute to get settled.

"Look who is here," I said with enthusiasm.

Schleifer had always welcomed her guests with a boisterous tone.

"Oh! It's *you*!" she would say, conveyed with a smile equal to her energetic voice. I did my best to provide a similar energy for Anne and David.

"Take a few breaths and show gratitude for each other's willingness to move the relationship forward. Thank each other with your eyes. Be grateful to be alive. Look at the photo of who is also in the room with us. Remember that this is not just for you. It is for them, as well. What your children learn from you will be carried into their future."

Anne and David responded right on cue. I reminded them of the roles of the visitor and the host. I reviewed the script, reminding David to use words sparingly, no more than five or six. Anne seemed a bit nervous, but both leaned forward as I had taught them and settled in quickly to their positions, 18 inches apart from each other.

David's opening words were purposeful and gentle.

"Anne, I would like to invite you to my neighborhood on a street called fear."

Anne took a few moments to respond.

"What I heard you say is that you want to invite me to your neighborhood on a street called fear. Am I with you?"

"Yes."

I nodded to Anne to respond with the words of the visitor.

"Tell me more."

"I'm scared when you disrespect our budget."

"What I heard you say is that you get scared when I disrespect our budget. Am I with you?"

"Yes. I feel you are not my partner."

"What I heard you say is that you feel that I am not your partner. Am I with you?"

"Yes.

Anne and David stayed focused on each other as these words passed between them. When they needed reminding, I used one finger to steer their eyes on each other. On several occasions, Anne did not respond exactly as David had spoken. Each time she did that I had David repeat his words until Anne repeated them accurately and to his satisfaction. Quite often, we added in our own language, but the object of this ritual is for one partner to learn the language of the other so that each can feel understood.

"When you don't stay in our budget, I get angry," David said. "I feel as though you don't know the value of money."

"What I heard you say," said Anne, "is that when I don't stay within our budget, you get angry because you don't feel that I know the value of money. Am I with you?"

David nodded.

"Yes. It worries me because it puts a financial strain on me."

"What I heard you say is that it worries you because it creates a financial strain on you. Am I with you?"

The host and visitor continued on this path until David's fear actualized.

"I'm scared Anne. I don't want us to be poor. You are going to drive us into the poor house."

This might seem contrived and staged, but it is neither. The purpose is to listen with every ounce of mindfulness the visitor can demonstrate, so the host feels heard and understood. There is no dialogue or questions, only the words in the script I taught them to use. I stay with them, encouraging them to stay focused as I allow them to proceed without interruption. If they import something illegal from their own neighborhood I stop the process and remind them to take it back. It is not an easy ritual, as the visitor is not always as mindful and present as we might prefer. However, when practiced and rehearsed it can create new neuro-pathways that will elicit a connection, which both partners have been missing.

David Goes Deeper

David stayed with the process, not just with his words, but through the heightened pitch of his feelings. As the ritual continued, his anger seemed to grow and when it reached a peak, I felt compelled to step in to ask a question.

"When in your childhood were you afraid of being poor?"

As David sat silently, tears emerged, even though he tried to hold them back. One leg began to shake.

"We were poor when my mother left my father. They divorced when I was only a year old. I was scared that she was going to send me away because she didn't have money to take care of me. She told me this as soon as I had the ability to understand it."

The tears continued to pour out like an open faucet.

"She told me she couldn't pay the bills and that I might have to live with my grandma." More tears.

"She cried at night and I didn't know what to say or do."

The child in David came out as he gave full expression to the fear he had held inside for so many years. In contrast, Anne came from a wealthy family, the daughter of a prominent banker and a mother who never had to work. Anne had no worries about not having enough to eat or being sent away. Her family enjoyed an abundance of riches and she had everything she wanted growing up. Money, or the lack of it, was never in her lexicon.

Anne stood frozen, tears rolling down her cheeks, as she kept her eyes on David. She was now witnessing the child who still resided within the man she married. It was as if a new light suddenly went off in her mind. Anne had always become angry whenever David confronted her about the things she bought for the house or their children. She never saw it as being spoiled or inconsiderate. In fact, from her perspective, Anne thought she was careful with money. David was adamant about not allowing her parents to subsidize any aspect of their life, so Anne had to learn to tighten her belt and be more conscious of what she spent.

Anne Sees David in a New Light

The ritual in my office presented a new paradigm shift for Anne. Watching David's essence emerge made her more empathic to his fear of being poor. Until now, she could never understand why he was so frugal or why he seemed to feel so contemptuous. David was a good provider, earning more six figures a year. They had just bought an expensive home and were living quite comfortably.

Anne was not fully aware of David's early childhood trauma—until now. His story hit her like a bolt of lightning. Until this moment she had always felt that David was demanding, unreasonable and uncompromising. She would describe his behavior as "my way or the highway." She felt that he could be incorrigible and suspected that he might even have a borderline personality disorder.

Anne had never met the authentic David. He was always wearing his survival suit. Suddenly, after nine years of marriage, the real David revealed himself. Anne, who had never seen him cry or lose his tough composure, was now seeing him as genuinely vulnerable. In these moments, she felt his pain, his worry and his suffering.

The ritual was not over, however, as we continued into my favorite part. We needed a corrective experience for David so I began to share what comes next.

"Anne, you are going to tell David a story as if he were a little boy. Tell him we now live in the 21st century where we have time machines. You are going to take David back to where he lived as a little boy and you are going with him."

They both seemed perplexed but stayed with me.

"Where did you live when you were a little boy, David?"

"I lived here, in Miami."

"Do you remember your address?"

"Yes, I do. It was 25 Cedar Street."

"Oh, that's North Miami Beach or Aventura, right?"

"Yes, it is."

I knew the neighborhood. Even 30 years ago it was an upper-middle class part of the area. David's family could not have lived there if they had been impoverished in any way. When his mother was left on her own, with a child to raise, her fear-based language and tone about their finances made David feel terribly insecure. Her words ran deep into his tender and unprotected brain. As an innocent and vulnerable child, he had no way of understanding their situation or the tools to see it from an adult perspective. David, like most children, absorbed the feelings of his primary parent, which left him feeling responsible for his imagined poverty. Even worse, he didn't have any resources to fix the problem. These primordial feelings stayed with him throughout his adult life and rose up unexpectedly during his marriage. Anne was just being herself. She had no clue about David's terror. She always assumed he was a strong man, fully capable of earning a good living and basically fearless. Hearing his story was shocking to her.

"Okay, Anne. Are you ready to take David in the time machine back to visit his mother at 25 Cedar Street in North Miami Beach?"

"Yes, yes I am. I will. Absolutely."

Anne had a sensitivity that David never realized she possessed. Throughout their marriage, they had both been living in their survival suits. Neither one of them ever really knew the other, not in the deepest ways that this ritual can reveal. Now, in my office, Anne finally understood why David was always twisting his hair and shaking his foot.

"What you are going to do is take David to the home where he once lived. When you land there and park the time machine, you will knock on the door. His mother will answer and you will introduce yourself. It will sound something like this: 'Hello Mrs. Ellis. My name is Anne and I am your daughter-in-law. I am from your future and I've come here with David to have a talk with you.' She will be curious so don't worry about her shutting the door in your face. Tell her that you married her son and that you have two children. You can give her their names if you so choose. Then you proceed to tell her what you have learned about David and his fear of being poor. Choose your words, not mine. Be as creative as you like. Are you ready?"

Anne seemed excited. She looked at David with a different set of eyes.

"I am ready."

After a few moments to collect her thoughts she spoke.

"David, I am going to take you on a special trip, one you have never known in your entire life. It's a trip to your past, and the best part is we are going to travel in a time machine. We are in the 21st century and I happen to have one right outside."

Anne looked at David when she offered him the trip. She instantly knew exactly what to say and how to behave. After all, she was the mother of two children, both under the age of eight, and had read several books on parenting. She took on the role as if she had rehearsed it many times.

"Are you ready to come with me?"

Her affect changed to that of a mother talking to a child. Her words were couched in gentle tones and her language matched her affect.

"Are you sure you want to do this?" said David. "You know my mother. She may not be as open as you hope."

They both chuckled. Still holding hands, they leaned closer into each other.

"You may be right, but I think I can handle her. Are you ready to go?"

David nodded with a smile.

"Okay, if that's what you want."

Anne made sounds of a rocket zooming through the air. When she landed, she used the table adjacent to their chairs and knocked three times. Her imagination made the visit seem like a fairytale and David was sucked right in. Knock, knock, knock, once more. Anne acted as if David's mother answered and she was primed to begin their encounter.

"Hello Mrs. Ellis. You don't know me, but one day in the future I am going to marry your son. My name is Anne. It was Anne Housman, but now it's Anne Ellis. I heard a lot about you from your son and I think it's time you and I had a visit. This is David. He's a grown man now and the father of your two grandchildren. I am sure you are going to meet them one day. Today, I came to share some important information with you. May I come in?"

Anne continued to stay in her role as if she had done this hundreds of times. It always amazed me to see how creative partners can be in this work. I give them little direction and they take off like a pro. She continued, as if they were together inside the house that had once been David's home.

"David told me it was really difficult growing up with you. He always felt like you were worried about money and that there was never enough. He told me he had the impression that you were going to send him away to live with his grandmother. He developed a great fear of abandonment due to this situation, so money and abandonment have been the core of his wounds until now. I am not sure why you conveyed this message to him, but it had residual effects throughout his childhood and adolescence, and they have remained until now. He always felt threatened and lived in silence with his fears. It has interfered with our marriage because he always feels that I will abandon him, due to his perceived inability to provide for me and our kids. Your words, intentional or not, left him with a fear of impoverishment and abandonment, even until today. They have impacted our marriage and I need you to apologize to him and release him from these fears. You may not have realized the damage you installed, and I'm sure you did not do it on purpose, but you can make amends. It's not too late."

It always amazes me to hear the way women are able to improvise so easily. They embellish the story to give it more power and understanding for their partner. David never had an advocate in his youth to reassure him about his security. Anne was now his champion. Listening to her share his repressed feelings registered an "Aha" moment in his mind. It was as though someone understood his pain. It was a relief to hear the words, which had never been in his consciousness, let alone been expressed. He sat silently, listening to Anne until she finished.

"David, is there anyone else you want me to talk to?"

"Yes, my father, but he doesn't live here. He lives in Hawaii."

"No big deal. The time machine is in the front yard. We can zip over to Hawaii in seconds. Let's go!"

The dialogue was repeated when they reached Hawaii. David knew his father's address, and when they landed in his front yard Anne repeated her introduction.

David's father had married his mistress, which was the reason for the divorce. He was quite wealthy and lived a glamorous lifestyle.

His two boys, both with his second wife, enjoyed the benefits of a rich daddy! Anne knew that David had been fatherless for most of his childhood, but David had always left out the deep emotions that had triggered, probably because he was, for the most part, not in touch with them. There was always a bravado attached to his story, which is common when we never remove our survival suits.

David had always felt abandoned by his father but tended to idealize him, as he was the absent parent. Although David would visit his father and new family, he felt unwanted, as if he never belonged there, and he was always relieved when it was time to go home. His issues of abandonment, plus his fear of not being able to fix things for his mother, left David feeling unwanted and helpless. This remained deep inside him until now.

This glimpse into David's life was not uncommon. In fact the movie, *Rocketman*, portraying the life story of Elton John, exemplifies David's life in many ways. Elton John's rocky relationship with his father revealed the same sense of abandonment and lack of a secure attachment. He felt that he didn't matter, and as a result he sought love and approval throughout his life, often in the wrong places. In many ways, this mirrored David's life, especially when Elton's father had two more sons with his second life, giving them what had been denied to Elton. The movie reflected that Elton John has done a lot of therapy with the Inner Child as part of his recovery.

Back in my office, it was time to visit Hawaii. Knock, knock knock! Once more the door opened and Anne pretended that a young male servant answered. She and David had been there many times with their children so she knew about his father's valet. Anne announced herself and requested to speak to Mr. Ellis. She told David that the valet had answered the door and was inviting them in. Just then, Anne acted as if David's father had entered the room.

"Oh, hello, Mr. Ellis. I am Anne, from your future. One day, I will marry your son, David, and become your daughter-in-law. Do you mind if I have a seat? I want to talk to you."

The scene was a repeat except for the dialogue, which was specific to the relationship regarding David and his father. Anne shared her understanding of how David's father's departure, and the fact that he chose to live so far away, had affected David, notwithstanding the impact his new wife and half-brothers had on his life.

While Anne spoke with authority and ease relating to the consequences of this on David, he began to sob, as if he were literally in his father's home. Anne's words had registered deeply with David and neither he nor Anne had ever experienced this behavior. I placed my hand between them as a reminder to allow the feelings to rise and fall until the wave crested. This took a few moments, all in silence, but when it was over, David looked at Anne with swollen eyes and a sense of peace and satiation. Anne had created a corrective experience for David simply by saying the words he could never share. This was because up until now he was not fully aware of how painful the loss of his father had been, and also because he would have never been able to recite the words that came so easy to Anne. Once again, she was his champion.

Reaching the Other Side

Anne and David crossed the bridge over troubled waters and reached the shore, where they could begin a process of genuine healing. The ritual continued with appreciations and precise words to describe the space between them. David shared his appreciation to Anne and let her know that he felt she was a true partner. Anne said that what she appreciated most was David's vulnerability. Each word described an aspect of their healing. They looked at each other with new eyes and a sense of deep, mutual understanding.

"See the new landscape in your partner's face," I said. "Look who's here. It's you, my husband. It's you, my wife."

We took some time to process the experience of Anne as the visitor and David as the host. Before the ritual began, David was hopeful that he could use this as an opportunity to express his discontent and anger with Anne. He imagined that she would not be able to defend her position, as that would have been an illegal import. In his own model of reality it would be a time for him to discharge his anger and resentment without her responding to his monologue. What he learned instead was that content doesn't matter in this work. It's all about the process. There is no blame, only revelation. We need to know what happened to us as children. Intentions do not matter!

After crossing the bridge over troubled waters and reaching the shore to heal, Anne and David were ready to continue with a new sense of hope. This ritual had taken the entire morning to complete. We stopped for lunch and continued until our time was up. David had more he needed to process. He had unfinished business with both parents, which he wanted to address. We spent the afternoon having both his parents, one at a time, do a ritual called *The Child Speaks to the Parent*. In this process, David, using a child's simple language, tells his parents what it was like growing up with them—what hurt him the most and which needs had not been met. With Anne playing the role of each parent, this created an opportunity for David to receive reparations from his parents. Taken together with what had transpired earlier, this became yet another bridge crossing over troubled waters, ultimately allowing Anne and David to arrive safely—and together—on the shores of healing.

What Do We Do Now?

My intention in this book is not to go through every principle and ritual I use in my practice. Instead, I prefer to illustrate the conflicts that arise in most relationships, with the understanding that many of the issues we face are a result of childhood traumas, which often slip through the cracks of our unconscious brain and lodge there until conflict arises later in life.

This is why Hedy Schleifer calls conflict an opportunity and a friend. When a couple learns how to apply this method to their relationship, they will discover that more than likely these conflicts arise out of unresolved childhood issues desperately trying to be resolved. The relationship is the platform where we can observe how these issues manifest. They play out in the here and now with the unconscious intention of healing the past, without our knowledge or awareness. That is why Freud called this *repetition compulsion* and Alice Miller referred to it as *The Logic of Absurdity*. We unconsciously hire our mates to help us understand and resolve childhood wounds, then we fire them for doing exactly what we hired them to do.

Therein lies the logic of absurdity. It's my job to call this out and lead my couples across the bridge. Your only job, if you are in need of any help, is to be willing to accept it.

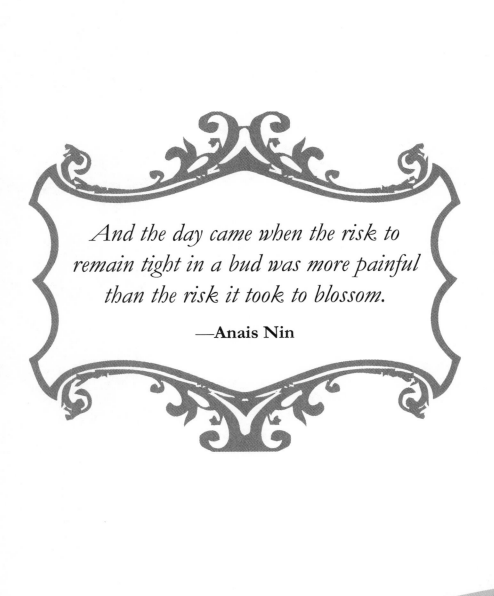

*And the day came when the risk to
remain tight in a bud was more painful
than the risk it took to blossom.*

—Anais Nin

8

Take Charge of Your Fears and Reclaim Your Value

Why is it so difficult for us to own our own stuff? Is defending ourselves more important than being clean and honest?

Was Socrates right when he said, "A life unexamined is not a life worth living?"

You already know the answers to these questions, but let me remind you about why you are right.

When we remain in a defensive mode, unwilling to come clean about how we feel, we are storing up layers of shame and/or guilt, and we may not even be aware that we are doing this. These feelings may be so buried in our sub-conscious that our automatic default position is to become defensive.

This behavior is prompted by the oldest and most primitive part of our brain—the reptilian, "fight or flight" mechanism. The only question this part ever asks is "Am I safe?" and "Will I survive?"

As we evolve, we take the elevator up to the neo-cortex and frontal lobe parts of our brain, which are the most recent parts of our known development. They ask reasonable and logical questions and help us work through why we feel the need to defend ourselves. The frontal lobe, which resides in the forehead, processes what the neo-cortex is thinking.

In other words, it explores our thoughts and allows us to see our behavior as an observer. If we allow ourselves to mature and be introspective, we challenge our own thinking and work through any negative behaviors we may have.

This process is essential in order to achieve healthy, adult relationships.

Defense Mechanisms

We all employ unconscious psychological strategies to protect us from anxiety, which can arise from unacceptable thoughts or feelings when we seem to be threatened, but defense mechanisms often get in our own way. According to Freud, when they become habitual they can result in neurosis, such as states of anxiety, phobias, obsessions or hysteria—for *both* genders.

You know them and you use them. In relationships they are your weapons of protection, but in fact they do not protect you. They can easily become weapons of mass destruction in the context of a relationship. They are a natural part of the human condition, at least until we learn how to shed our survival suits. Then, and only then, can we evolve to a higher consciousness and discover our authentic selves—who we really are. As long as we continue to maintain our false selves, we cannot learn how to resolve conflict.

In previous chapters, I discussed our survival suits and how we hold on to our false selves in order to survive—or so we think. Honestly, inhabiting these defense mechanisms ultimately get us nowhere. What worked in our childhood no longer works when we are trying to create and maintain healthy relationships, not just with our partners, but with friends, children, business associates, and colleagues. The only thing that really works is to be in our essence.

Here is a list of defense mechanisms and what they do to protect us:

Denial

This is one of the most common responses we use to defend ourselves. This refusal to accept reality is meant to avoid emotional pain, but it ultimately blocks us from becoming aware of the truth—and working our way toward acceptance.

Repression

This occurs when unpleasant thoughts, painful memories, or irrational beliefs are driven down into the sub-conscious corners of our brain.

Projection

We do this when we attribute unwanted thoughts, feelings and motives onto another person. In inter-personal relationships, the easiest way to discharge our unacceptable parts is to project them onto our partner.

Displacement

When we redirect an impulse onto a powerless substitute target, too often our partner, we are displacing our feelings and shirking responsibility.

Regression

This occurs when we feel threatened or stressed and our behavior reverts to an earlier stage of development, such as having a temper tantrum.

Rationalization

All too often, excuses are a way to justify our behavior.

Sublimation

We do this when we replace unacceptable emotions and behaviors with alternatives that are constructive and will satisfy the positive intention of our destructive urges. For example, teenagers with aggressive tendencies may channel their aggression into contact sports. Another example might be turning objectionable sexual impulses into music or art. That's when negative energy can be *sublimated* into positive behavior.

Reaction formation

This behavior occurs when a person attempts to hide his or her true feelings or desires by demonstrating or adopting the exact opposite feelings. It is used as a defense against anxiety, which can be caused by negative feelings.

Identification with the Aggressor

We see this when hostages establish an emotional bond with their captors, such as during a kidnapping, or when a child identifies with an aggressive parent and develops similar behavior.

While this chapter is not intended to be a text book for Psych 101, recognizing what defense mechanisms you and your partner use can help both of you to better understand your behavior and how it affects your relationship.

The Value of Owning Your Dark Side and Making Amends

What is the dark side of a human personality? Carl Jung referred to it as our shadow side. According to Jung, our shadow, instinctive and irrational, is prone to psychological projection, when a perceived personal inferiority is recognized as a perceived moral deficiency in someone else. It's that part that we don't want to own or realize that it exists. This part is reprehensible to us, so when we act out this part we often wonder why and where it came from. It's as if Jekyll and Hyde live inside us and we don't know why or what makes Hyde keep popping out.

Sometimes, our partner can trigger the worst in us. That occurs when it fires off earlier feelings of trauma, which may not be in our consciousness. We walk away feeling ashamed and guilty of our behavior, wondering what occurred to make us act in such an unsavory and reprehensible manner. When we recognize the original pain and/or trauma, we can better understand the cause, however, not the cure.

Remember Ellen?

When she had a melt down on her wedding night and broke a vase, her level of frustration had reached overdrive and she was unable to contain her anger. There were obvious reasons for her explosion, but if we dig a little deeper we can understand that she had collected stamps over many years from her family of origin. Her childhood, teenage years and early adulthood had been filled with volcanic material. When she was unable to receive any support from her brand new husband or her family she erupted—a result of her past frustrations and rage, along with the groom's lack of cooperation. She lost it, which gave her 30-hour husband a reason to have her Baker-Acted.

If we could re-write Ellen's life story and learn that she came from a healthy and supportive family, this cluster fuck of a wedding night may never have occurred. Then again, if that were true, she most probably would never have chosen Mark as her husband. She was repeating her past, with an unconscious desire to fix what had been broken.

I explained this in a previous chapter, but it bears repeating.

We unconsciously choose our mates to help us work through our childhood wounds. When they do exactly what we "hired" them to do, we fire them! This is why psychologist Alice Miller quotes it as the art of absurdity.

"If we do not work on all three levels—body, feeling, mind—the symptoms of our distress will keep returning, as the body goes on repeating the story stored in its cells until it is finally listened to and understood."

Sound familiar?

Ellen's mood reached a level where she could not contain her anger. Her inner Eliza Doolittle, masquerading in this case as "Hyde," lunged after her symbolic Henry Higgins, when she heaved his slippers with a force so unlike the person she had been trained to become. Ellen reached that level of frustration on her wedding day, which elicited her dark side (Hello Mr. Hyde), and she regressed in that moment of intense stress and had a temper tantrum.

In my model of the world, I would say her anger rose from feeling manipulated and controlled by her Svengali (Hello Mark), who was trying to morph her into someone she didn't want to be. Of course *My Fair Lady* was fictional, so I have no idea what Eliza's impoverished life might have been about, so I am unable to draw precise dots from her past to a conclusion. But in Ellen's case, we *can* see the arc of anxiety from her childhood to the altar.

Remember Margie?

She became so incensed when she discovered—one too many times—that her boyfriend had a harem he was using for his own private entertainment. Since Margie did not have direct access to her neo-cortex and frontal lobe, her inner Hyde exploded with a vengeance that manifested into physical violence when she pushed him into a closet and beat him relentlessly with her arms and legs. She walked away from that event feeling guilty and ashamed of her primitive behavior and lack of control. When we explored her history, it didn't take long to see that the frustration and anger she had displaced onto her partner was unconsciously intended for her father, who had abused her through his abandonment.

This had triggered her fear of poverty and confirmed the insecure attachment she had known since childhood. It was not the same behavior as Brad, her partner, but real feelings of betrayal were triggered and she was beating up both her father and Brad. In Margie's mind, she had been abandoned by both of them—her father for not providing financial security and Brad for his womanizing, putting her at risk with chronic heartache and the potential to contract a venereal disease.

This was a quintessential sado-masochistic relationship. Margie had chosen Brad to ensure that she would never be impoverished, but the payoff was perhaps worse. She lost herself in an attempt to create a secure attachment, which she had never experienced as a child.

I worked with Ellen and Margie to look into their dark side and explore why they made these choices, especially their unconscious choices, which were even more relevant than their conscious choices. That's because our behavior is dictated by the unconscious.

Ellen had lived with Mark for four years prior to their marriage. Margie had been with Brad for more than five years. Both women's behavior had not just revealed itself in one day, one week or one month. It had been obvious during the entire time these women had been together with their partners, with the exception of the courtship period, when everybody puts their best foot forward.

While observing the dark side of their partners, each of them continued to maintain the status quo, suffering disappointment after disappointment. The evidence was revealed over and over, yet they continued to maintain their relationships, thinking that they would be able to effect the improvements and changes they were seeing. In spite of their partner's predictable behavior, and even when they repeatedly cried their guts out, leaving the relationship was not an option for either one of them. Ellen and Margie were each addicted and feared being alone more than staying. They rationalized this reasoning, and this mind game won each time they felt disillusionment and heartache.

Ellen and Margie sold themselves a bill of goods.

Their insecure attachments and co-dependency allowed the status quo to remain. When nothing changed, Ellen thought marriage might be the answer. Margie had hoped for the same, even though marriage was not a consideration for Brad. He loved the status quo. Margie was the main event in his life, while his harem supplied his drug of choice. Margie remained, come hell or high water, and it was mostly hell—for her. She kept Brad grounded and stable, not unlike the role of a nurturing mother, but it was not fulfilling enough to undo his insatiable need to conquer women. This insatiable need of Brad's had a weird and damaging parallel in Margie's insatiable need to conquer him.

Brad used his money and charm to maintain his harem and his relationship with Margie. All of the women in his life seemed addicted to his life style and generosity. However, while the harem accepted his wanton desires in exchange for benefits he provided, that was not the case with Margie. She wanted more—nothing unreasonable, just fidelity and exclusivity—something Brad was not capable of giving her or any woman. Margie's efforts in attempting to convert him to exclusivity failed miserably, yet she hung in there. Her neurotic needs, a result of her insecure attachment in childhood, continued to fuel her co-dependency and addiction.

Ironically, Margie was a successful business woman. She had her own real estate agency, employing more than a dozen realtors. She earned way beyond six figures annually, yet because of her deep emotional wounds she didn't feel worthy without this man in her life. For some reason, her need to conquer Brad was insatiable. Nothing was ever enough. Brad was a player in the top one percent of America's wealthy elite, and Margie was willing to sell her soul to the devil to be a part of it.

What we know in psychology is that you can't fix an internal problem with an external solution. It never works!

As Albert Einstein said, "No problem can be solved from the same level of consciousness that created it."

For Ellen and Margie, the only way out of their relationships would come through denying their denial. They had to come clean because their mental and physical health were at risk. After months of intensive therapy, Margie was able to break the co-dependency and move on. Ellen had no choice. Mark asked for an annulment, but their 30-hour marriage ended in divorce. That didn't mean that all was well. It was the beginning of a new and painful journey for both women and each of them had a lot to learn about themselves, especially how their dark sides had been keeping them out of the light. As we know, childhood wounds run deep and the consequences of that damage can affect other relationships. The lesson is, if you don't embrace your shadow side, it will bite you in the ass!

Healing the Wound and Finding Closure

There are occasions when crossing the bridge to resolve childhood wounds will work for individuals as well as couples. Although there are multiple spins we can put on the process, the results can often be rewarding. Here is an example of how I was able to work with a woman who had been abandoned by her father since birth and how she was able to come to closure.

For nearly a year, Katie had been ruminating about seeking professional help. Her best friend, Alicia, convinced her to schedule an appointment. Katie is an attractive 46-year-old, happily married women with three teenage children. Kim is 17, James is 15 and Andrew just turned 13. Katie's conflict was not about her marriage or her children, although it frequently interfered with both aspects of her life.

Katie had been abandoned by her biological father before her birth because he did not want to be a part of her life. He never married Katie's mother and chose not to have anything to do with his child. Although he surfaced occasionally, he never recognized his daughter and denied any responsibility for her. Soon after Katie was born, her mother married, and Katie's step-father adopted her and became Dad. As soon as she was able to comprehend the facts of her birth, Katie was told about her biological father. Her parents had two more children and even though they were half-brothers, Katie never felt like an outsider. She was treated as if they were all born to the same parents. Even so, her feelings of worthlessness remained lodged in a deep corner of her mind. The rejection and abandonment she felt defined her as not being lovable.

It was difficult for Katie to share these feelings. The uncertainty surrounding her biological father's abandonment and disinterest in her life left a hole in her soul with its unfinished business. Although grateful to her adopted father for raising her with love and support, she still did not know why her biological father had chosen estrangement. Katie knew where he was and how to contact him, but she avoided any effort to connect. She could never bring herself to confront her feelings of being fatherless. She defended her feelings by pretending not to care. She even told me she hated him.

"What kind of a man denies his daughter her birthright?" she said. "He's a piece of shit, a dog and I hate him. He doesn't deserve me. I've managed to become strong and independent without his love and support. Why should I give a shit now? It's his loss. He didn't deserve to have me as his daughter."

Katie began to sob. I waited for the wave of despair to settle. She looked at me for understanding and compassion. I said nothing but stayed connected with soft eyes.

"Then why did you seek therapy?"

"I'm not sure. These feelings of rejection have been pervasive throughout my life. They sometimes interfered with my marriage, my work and my relationship with my mother. I couldn't talk to her about this because she wouldn't understand. She would say 'Why do you even care? You have a Dad that loves you and has taken care of you since you were a baby.' I ran into the same response with my siblings, my aunt and even my friends. His lack of interest and dismissal defined me as not being worthy. It impacted my self-esteem and I pretended it didn't matter. But it was me that felt I didn't matter."

We sat in silence for a moment.

"I hate him," she said, over and over, with genuine contempt.

I had Katie cross the bridge to express her feelings of abandonment and the impact it had made on her life. She was reluctant to do the process, fearing she would lose her composure. She had been able to mask her feelings with indifference, exchanging her need for love with hate and dismissal, as he had done with her. This was a reaction to her authentic feelings of wanting to be loved and accepted by the father she never knew. Finally, she shared her story of growing up without her biological father, and the feelings of rejection soon caused tears to emerge.

"I don't think I can do this. It's too painful."

I aligned myself with her fear.

"Yes, I am sure it is very painful. Do you want to heal and get closure?"

"I'm not sure. I don't know if it will help. I feel I have lived well all my life without his presence, so why would I want to open wounds that I have kept closed all my life?"

Her fear was palpable. She took several tissues from the box while her tears and visible discomfort reinforced the pain she had been repressing all of her life.

"In order to heal, the wounds you have kept closed all your life must be opened and discharged so that you can have closure. Your father is not here, so in essence, he can't reject you. What's his name?"

Katie hesitated for a long time, which I allowed her to do. Finally, she spoke, as tears spilled down her cheeks.

"S…S…Sam."

"Okay, let's put Sam in the chair."

I set up two chairs facing each other, as I do when I have couples crossing the bridge. "Sam will be seated in one and you in the other. Are you with me?"

"I guess so."

"I am going to teach you how to cross the bridge to meet Sam, your biological father."

"What if I can't do it? What if I don't like what he says? I don't want to learn why he didn't value me as his daughter."

"That won't happen."

I tried to reassure her that it was time to address these repressed feelings, that this would be a key to her recovery.

"This takes courage, Katie. This is why you made the appointment to see me, even if a part of you did not want to come. Another part knew what you needed to do, so you made the choice to work through this. Do you want to finally heal this wound?"

Katie nodded, and sat in the chair I had reserved for her.

"Your father, Sam, is seated in the empty chair in front of you. He is here now, waiting to hear your voice. Imagine his presence. Imagine how he looks. This is your chance for change. I will be with you every step of the way."

I encouraged Katie to use her imagination to see her father. I reminded her that she knows what he looks like because it was only recently that she saw him at the home of a relative. She had seen him many times over the years, and each time he fell silent to her presence or left the room. He had always been uncomfortable to face her. Now, with his presence occupying a chair across form Katie, he would become a willful participant.

"Look at your father and tell him what it was like never having known him."

This time there was no hesitation.

"Oh my God!" she cried. "It was awful. I couldn't get you out of my mind, always wondering why—why you didn't care—why you never tried to see me—why you ran away from your responsibilities as a father—why you didn't love me. How could you? I was just a baby, not even born yet—your baby, and yet you never showed up. I felt like I didn't exist and that I didn't matter."

Katie paused as her tears morphed into sobs, mixing with guttural sounds bellowing from her core.

I waited for the wave of sobs to subside before I began again.

"Tell him how he hurt you."

Katie blew her nose and wiped her tears. She took a couple of breaths and sat frozen, unable to speak. I waited silently until she composed herself.

"Tell him how he hurt you."

Katie took a few more breaths and wiped her red and swollen eyes.

"You hurt me. You denied my existence. I needed to know you loved me and cared about me, but you never showed up. Damn you!

What is wrong with you? What kind of a man are you? You're a loser, a coward, a miserable piece of shit, and I hate you. I hate you! I hate you! I hate you!"

"Tell him what you needed most from him that he didn't give you. Go ahead, tell him. He's right here in front of you. Tell him."

I had raised my voice to a pitch she had not heard before.

"I needed you to acknowledge me—to see me, hear me, know that I am your child, your daughter, but you never did. You stayed away like a coward, a loser, denying the love I needed and pretended I didn't. You made me feel invisible, like I didn't matter."

I reached over and grabbed a piece of pipe I keep for moments like this. Katie began to reveal her anger. The color of her face changed to match her anger. I handed her the pipe and said bring it down. It didn't take more than a moment before the pipe slammed hard onto the chair that housed her father.

"Bring it down, Katie. Say 'I'm angry!'"

I shouted this to her to give her permission to express her anger.

"Bring it down with force! Let him know how angry you are for abandoning you. Bring it down and say the words, 'I'm angry, I'm angry.'"

Soon the pipe slammed hard against the chair where her father had been sitting.

"You left me. You ran away like a coward, a miserable coward."

Katie was screaming as she continued to use force with the pipe. "More sound. Louder!"

She swung the pipe harder and harder, giving her voice the power she had repressed for so long, defending the denial of her feelings. Her anger mounted with each swing. Again and again, she shouted.

"I'm angry, I'm angry, I'm angry!"

Katie kept shouting until she was physically exhausted. She took several breaths, then tossed the pipe onto the sofa. She looked at me, overwhelmed, but seemingly grateful. I waited a few minutes as her breathing returned to normal.

"How do you feel?"

"Tired, but relieved. I don't like expressing anger, as it's not the way I was raised. I feel lighter and somewhat liberated. Wow—I guess I've been holding on to my anger for a long time, a long time, way too long."

"Yes, you have, and now you gave your child, little Katie, a voice she never knew she had. You are her champion. What you needed from your father that you never got was his love, his acceptance and his acknowledgment that you are his daughter, his little girl."

There were more tears, but this time they seemed to be tears of joy instead of sorrow. Katie, the adult and child still within her, looked at me and smiled.

"Thank you. Thank you for setting me free. You see, anger is not a feeling that is acceptable in my family. Actually there are many feelings that are not acceptable. Sadness, anger and fear are never expressed. If I dared to show anger, I was told it was a sin. If I was sad, my father would say, 'I'll give you something to be sad about.' If I was afraid, I was told there was nothing to be afraid of. I was shamed if I showed these feelings, so I learned early in my life not to express them."

"Instead, you became split off from what you were told were negative and unacceptable feelings. I guess you buried them, along with your father."

Then I recited a quote I had on a large chart in my office, which I had memorized over my many years in practice.

"If you bring forth what is within you, what you bring forth will save you. If you do not bring forth what is within you, what you do not bring forth, will destroy you."

Katie looked at me with the face of an innocent child. There was a sense of curiosity and wonder in her now, showing on her face, as if she just had a revelation or epiphany.

"This is a quote from Jesus."

We both sat in silence as she processed the work she had just completed.

"I want you to close your eyes and see little Katie, the baby girl who was abandoned by her father."

Katie closed her eyes and followed my instructions.

"Ask her to come forward so you can see her face. You know exactly what she looks like. Notice everything about her—her eyes, the way she wears her hair, the clothes she has on and especially her eyes. Imagine you can pick her up and put her on your lap and hold her right here in your arms."

As I instructed Katie to hold her child in her lap, I placed a teddy bear in her arms, leaned over and gently placed her arms around the teddy bear.

"Tell her how precious she is—how special-- that there has never been anyone like her before and there would never be anyone like her again. Tell her she is lovable, smart and beautiful. You don't need to say these words aloud, only with your heart. She will hear you. Tell her that of all the people she will meet in her life, you are the only one who will never leave her."

Katie began to cry. She hugged the teddy bear, now a symbol of the child within her. The tears falling were bringing her to a sense of closure and completion. It was now up to her to take care of her little girl, the child that had been abandoned and denied the love she had needed. Katie would have to be the champion this child never had.

What Do We Do Now?

I've worked with so many women still suffering as adults from the harm they experienced as children. Each one of them need a special form of TLC to break through the logjam of emotions, which had been holding them back for so long.

In Katie's case, she hated the man she wanted to love, the man she had wanted to love her back without conditions. Her hate was a reaction to the love she had been denied. Her religious training and upbringing had fostered an environment of repressing her feelings—until I gave her permission to release them. Once that happened, the hurt beget the anger. Katie's healing began by honoring the feelings she had not been able to express.

I asked Katie to write a letter to her father, which she didn't have to send. I asked her to write down all the feelings she had harbored silently for so long. This was an assignment to bring for her next appointment the following week.

"I wrote the letter. It was hard to do, but once I began typing, the words fell onto my fingers without any effort. They just appeared on the screen as if someone else wrote them."

"That's because you released your truth last week with me as your benign witness. Can you read it to me?"

Katie opened the letter and began.

"Dear Sam….."

The poetic letter was written with heartfelt feelings of grief and despair, like a song of woe. As Katie read through the pages her tone began to change. Her voice was no longer shadowed by sobs. It resonated with strength as she enunciated each word with conviction. Occasionally, she took a deep breath and paused. A few tears emerged, but Katie stayed with the words she had written. Every word came from her limbic system, the seat of emotion in the brain, the part she had cut off to protect herself. Now those feelings were free to surface and her words were the tool to give her back her power.

I listened with a sense of gratitude. We had transformed her life to a place of freedom. I felt like a great quarterback, and Katie was a star wide receiver. It had taken both of us to create this transformational experience. Her business was not finished. This was only the first chapter.

"Now, if you feel strong, it would be a good idea to meet with Sam and share your letter. It's your call, but I would encourage you to do this."

"What if he won't meet with me? What if he avoids it?"

"Let's cross that bridge when we get there. One baby step at a time. Do you know how to reach him?"

"Yes, that's not a problem. I can get his number from my aunt. I just need to think this through. I don't know if I'm ready."

"Take your time. You've waited this long. You have to feel ready, Katie. I trust you can do this."

Katie looked at me and nodded.

"Yes, you are right. This is the last step of my journey."

"I am glad you see it that way. Even if you never read the letter to him, you have done an amazing amount of work. You are a warrior! You have a goddess in you who can take you across the finish line. Her name is Athena. She is an archetypal energy that resides within you."

Katie understood. No more words were necessary. She now felt empowered to do what she had to do.

A week later, Katie returned, a bit bubbly, but still composed. She took a seat on the sofa and told me that she'd had a very good week. She felt resolved and complete. I wasn't ready for what was to come. As I listened to her, I noticed her undeniable joy.

"What's going on?"

"I spoke to Sam. I told him I wanted to meet with him. He said he has been waiting for this moment all his life. We met a few days ago, on Tuesday."

"Wow! How did you feel?"

"Shocked, but excited and even hopeful. I wasn't sure he was going to show up. I expected him to call with an excuse to cancel, but he didn't."

According to Katie, Sam came into Starbucks, their designated meeting spot. As soon as he saw her, he put his arms around her and began to tremble.

"Katie, I waited for this moment all my life, never believing it would happen. How brave of you to reach out to me. I haven't been there for you. I thought this day would never come."

They both began to tear up.

Katie said that Sam owned up to his behavior and how he had abandoned her. He felt ashamed, and the more the years passed, the more ashamed he felt. She spoke his words as if she had memorized everything he said to her.

"'I know I failed you,' he told me. 'Reasons won't matter now. I was stupid, a stupid jerk. I ran away from you, your mother and all my responsibilities. By the time I realized what I had done, the shame I felt made me stay away longer. The few times I saw you I couldn't even look in your eyes. I guess I was a bad guy, a lousy father, and as time went on I was too afraid to face you. You were the one who suffered due to my behavior. If you hadn't reached out to me, I might have gone my whole life never having this moment with you or the chance to say I'm sorry.'"

Katie continued to detail the conversation. Her words in response to his made me feel that she had attained the closure she had been longing for all this time.

"I guess you were right," she said.

"That's not important, Katie. *You* did this! You did what you thought was right. You took care of yourself and little Katie. You made her feel that she mattered. You are, and always will be, her champion."

Katie's closure opened the door to other wounds she wanted to heal. Her success with her father gave her the belief that if she could do that and get the results she had hoped for, then she had no reason to hide behind her fears any longer. She could do anything. Her newfound empowerment over-shadowed any of the anxiety she had of opening up other wounds.

Katie reminded me of the beauty of this process. I have always told my clients that when a person decides to commit, the universe cooperates!

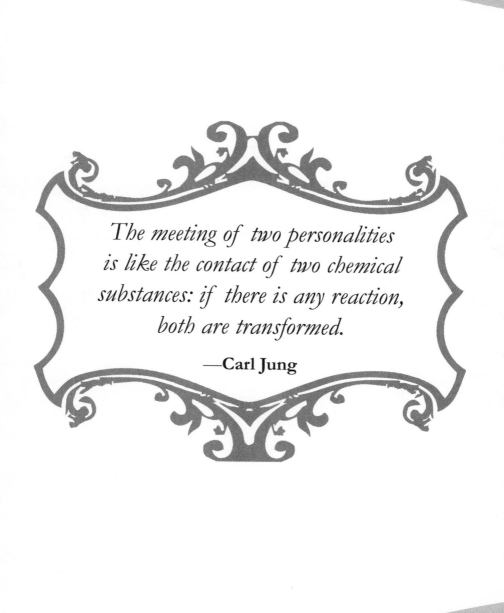

The meeting of two personalities
is like the contact of two chemical
substances: if there is any reaction,
both are transformed.

—Carl Jung

9

Where, Oh Where, Has My Sexy Self Gone?

Every relationship and marriage has its ups and downs. Sometimes, the downs can last longer and do more damage than a partnership can tolerate. Even so, with the proper tools and resources, couples *can* learn to recognize and communicate their differences, negotiate healthy compromise and navigate through those stormy times, often preventing a break-up because they made a loving and sincere effort to find solutions.

One of the most common problems men and women encounter is sexual dysfunction, which can happen, even out of the blue, at any age. In women, this is usually a symptom of another underlying issue, which may be apparent or is lurking somewhere under the surface.

Why Is This Happening?

Sexual dysfunction can be due to *intra*-personal reasons, such as anxiety, depression, stress, poor body image, a history of low self-esteem because of earlier physical and/or sexual abuse, and unresolved anger. Any of these issues can manifest themselves unwittingly—and at any time—into a woman's relationship.

Sexual dysfunction, and all the conflict it brings, can also be due to *inter*-personal reasons, which are often unresolved issues within a relationship that usually trigger wounds from the past. Mental and physical illness, as well as attitudes and beliefs formed early in life, are important factors to consider when attempting to identify what is contributing to a loss of libido. There are many mitigating circumstances, which affect both women and men. Alcohol and drugs are a major contributor to sexual dysfunction, as is aging, medications, and excessive pornography. Addiction, whether it's alcohol, drugs or a behavior of choice, often fuels disconnection, which can undermine intimacy in a hurry. For example, it's not easy to give your man a blow job when you're harboring hostility, which has not been resolved. So there you have it! Just as a point of interest, human beings are not the only species who have sexual dysfunction.

More often than not, psychological reasons do not arise until a couple has either taken their vows or the relationship has progressed to building a family. After the honeymoon stage, the birth of a child can often interfere with the freedom that a couple used to enjoy. Once you add more kids, a woman will become even more exhausted from caring for the onslaught of what her extended family requires—let alone what her husband needs—so by the time she beds down with him for the night how can she have any energy left for sex?

Women who work, have kids and don't have any support to lighten their load, develop apathy toward having sex, and that's simply because of exhaustion and feeling alone in their effort to keep all of that together. Their energy is depleted from a full day at work, followed by meeting the needs of the children, doing housework, shopping, preparing dinner, tidying up and taking the dog for a walk. If their partners are supportive and share these responsibilities, there will be plenty of energy left for lovemaking. But if a woman must take on all these roles and responsibilities alone, sex will fall to the bottom of her To Do list and her sexual interest will flat line.

During this time, anger will probably build up, along with a dose of resentment, and sex will be compromised, most often without a conscious thought one way or another. In simple terms, under ideal circumstances life as a family requires two adults to handle all the responsibilities and obligations, especially these days when both parents are working. If housekeepers are affordable, this can remove some of the burden, especially for the woman, as long as both partners agree about hiring help.

A Shout Out to Single Mothers

I'm sure you know at least one divorced woman who is taking care of her kids largely by herself, working, and trying her best to meet her domestic responsibilities. All too often, she doesn't have the time or energy to enjoy a fulfilling sex life, so in time her sexuality will diminish or even disappear altogether.

Time management is the key to igniting these human needs.

Loneliness, when it becomes too deep, can be dangerous if it seeps into a woman's life and her need to connect becomes lost—all because of a lack of time and vitality. Even something supposedly handy, like exploring online dating, can end up in frustration, disappointment, and regret, especially because a bad date is a waste of valuable time!

Of course this is not always the case. I know many single and divorced women with children who have been successful in finding fulfilling relationships through a plethora of dating services. However, that usually takes quite a bit of time, patience, effort and a strong constitution and sense of humor. Rejection runs rampant in the world of online dating, for women and men, alike. After months and even years of searching for the right mate, giving up is not uncommon.

When the Fairytale Begins

During the initial stages of a courtship sex is vital to cement the relationship and often occupies most of the couple's time. Once we go between the sheets, we fall into a trance and projections fly everywhere. Magical thinking sweeps us off our feet. It takes us to the moon on gossamer wings, as we see and believe what might not even exist. This is nature's way of tricking us into procreating to make more of us, while we think our hot sex life is love!

During the honeymoon stage, everybody's singing their best tenor and soprano parts, enjoying the best parts of their romantic sexual aria. We've certainly seen this fantasy portrayed in many films, but life does not always imitate art. Unfortunately, sex drives fade and reality eventually sets in. What happens then is what really matters—after all that good lovin' has rocked our boats.

"Where is the man who ripped my clothes off, stayed for hours in bed, looking into my eyes and telling me how beautiful I am"?

I often hear this question in my sessions.

Suddenly, seemingly out of nowhere, without cause or affect, the person who shared your bed and couldn't get enough of you abruptly loses interest and the sexuality you once shared becomes yesterday's *Kelsey's nuts*. Once the conquest has been accomplished, your sensual, horny Mr. Wonderful becomes disinterested and stingy, as he falls asleep, leaving you to your own devices, and replacing hours of pillow talk with snoring.

In all fairness, men do not corner the market on this behavior, but still . . .

The Four Stages of a Relationship

Susan Campbell wrote that each stage of a relationship mimics each stage of human psychic development.

In the first stage, when we are infants, we look to our mothers for all our dependency needs. This stage is called *co-dependency*. It's the stage of "falling in love" when we are adults. All the boundaries collapse and we feel nothing but the magic and splendor of the newness of each other. Each partner's needs are met, not unlike how a baby and new mother meet the needs of each other. The baby looks into the eyes of the mother. The mother looks down into the eyes of the baby, and they share a feeling of being together as one. That's our first connection, which kind of repeats itself during the first stage of a romantic relationship, when we often hear a couple refer to each other as their "soulmate."

In the second stage of life, called *counter-dependency*, a child begins to move away from his or her mom and explores the world. This is the beginning of what psychologists call *individuation* and *separation*, two parts of our normal growth and development.

In relationships, we begin to adjust to the same changes. Boundaries begin to pop back up and each partner moves a little bit away from each other, noticing the differences rather than the sameness that was seen in the first stage. This is when many marriages and relationships fall apart, when the "soulmate" title is dropped and exchanged for labels like dog, asshole or jerk. It's tough to hang in there and go for a resolution because things begin to happen unconsciously, which we are not always in touch with or able to communicate. This is when some of our unresolved childhood issues surface and interface with what is occurring in our relationships. When our pasts collide with the present most of us don't have the conscious awareness, tools, skills, and resources to work it out.

Most people are not even aware of how their personal history contaminates their relationships. We grow up in homes with poor role modeling and use that as our frame of reference for how a relationship should be. We bring in our own set of family systems and unresolved conflicts with our parents and unconsciously want to work it out in our adult relationships. We end up repeating patterns from the only modeling we know.

Doing what comes naturally, however, is not necessarily in our best interest.

Without insight and understanding, we tend to fight it out, often times unfairly, using blaming, shaming, criticism, contempt, stonewalling and judgment. Most of this behavior we learned in our own homes. This inevitably causes a rift in the relationship, resulting in sexual disinterest and/or dysfunction. This is when most couples or individuals come into treatment, and many times it's already too late to repair the problem.

However, this is not always the case, and I have found that when we can discharge the pain, beliefs and hurts from the past, everyone has a chance to make a new start. This depends on the willingness of both parties to move forward, and if there is enough healthy tissue left to repair. Not every relationship is reparable. Sometimes, irreconcilable differences make it best if couples divorce or break up. Staying together for the sake of the children is not a sufficient reason, as they reap any unresolved conflicts inherited from their parents, setting them up to possibly reenact them all over again in their own adult relationships.

According to Erik Erikson, a social psychologist, the third state of human psycho/social development is called *initiative versus guilt*.

In relational development this means declaring independence, which begins in childhood, when we go to school and discover our autonomy and independence. It's our first time away from home, facing issues without Mom and Dad there to take care of things. As we learn to do this successfully, we grow more self-assured and build our self-esteem.

In relationships, there is no intimacy without autonomy.

When we reach this third stage in our relationships, not being needed as much as in the first and second stages can become a threat to our partners. The mental health and maturity of each partner will determine how well they work through this stage. It takes two healthy, mature adults to build and maintain a successful relationship, with each party free to enjoy their own autonomy. When co-dependency is the foundation of the relationship, it is doomed to fail unless both partners thrive equally in that co-dependency.

In 1492, Rabbi Mendell, a noted scholar of his time, said, "If I am I because I am I, and you are you because you are you, then I am and you are. But if I am I because you are you, and you are you because I am I, then I am not and you are not!" This wise man coined co-dependency more than 600 years ago.

The fourth stage is called *interdependence*. Fifty percent of couples never arrive here because more than half of all divorces take place in the second and third stage. It takes years for this fourth stage to mature, when each partner supports the autonomy of the other and enriches each other's life, rather than completes or competes with it. This requires genuine relational maturity, self-esteem, insight into owning our own stuff (described in the previous chapter), and becoming enlightened, what others may call *conscious* or in the slang of today, *woke*. It takes two woke people in a conscious relationship to succeed. Most couples require a therapist to help them arrive at this stage. The good news, it can be done!

Three Reasons Relationships Fail

Throughout these four stages, the most common reaction I see to the anger and hurt that arises in all relationships is getting "turned off." The only exception to this is when two people agree never to disagree, and that does not make for a conscious relationship. Most of the time, sexual dysfunction raises its nasty head as a result of this turn-off and it can happen equally to men and women. It is one manifestation of a relationship turned sour, which has become polluted over time. If this is the case, each party, within the structure of the relational space, has personal work to do so that they can resolve any issues they may have within their own family of origin, which they may have dragged from the past into their shared present.

Crossing the bridge is a useful platform to address this.

Most family of origin issues are socked away in gunny sacks that eventually become transported into the relationship. If these include abuse (physical, emotional, verbal, sexual, intellectual, or spiritual), abandonment or neglect, which was connected with either partner—and even worse, with both—then the relationship becomes "a killing field."

This is why it is so important that these matters be treated like a broken bone. Without proper treatment, and a real "re-set," they won't heal on their own and will surely get played out in the relational space, polluting and potentially destroying what was once so wonderful.

Most of us come into relationships with unrealistic expectations, and when they are not met by our significant other we soon face disappointment, disillusionment and bitterness. Not surprisingly, our libido diminishes as these expectations are not realized. Changing those expectations is paramount to a successful outcome.

Poor role modeling, unrealistic expectations and childhood trauma are perhaps the most common reasons why relationships fail.

The Curse of Technology

The onslaught of Viagra, Cialis, Levitra and other sexually stimulating drugs manufactured for men—with nothing yet that match them for women—has only widened the gap in the natural process of aging. Men can maintain their sexual prowess with the help of these drugs while women are left in their natural aging process without chemical support.

This has become a pandemic sexual issue in couples in their 50s and through the rest of their lives. While women are slowing down, men, with the assistance of pills and other sexual stimulants, are still behaving as if they are in their 20s, 30s and 40s, unless of course prostate problems arise, which levels the playing field. The aging factor, as it specifically pertains to sexuality, no longer insures compatibility.

Living in today's world, with all its stressors and variables that we cannot control, contributes to a lack of longevity in relationships. What used to be "forever, until death do us part" happens less than 60 percent of the time in marriages today. Technology has exhausted the human spirit, leaving many in chaos, just trying to keep up with the times. Our minds, and what constitutes our soulful content, cannot expand fast enough to keep up with the pace of technological innovations. We barely speak to each other. Email and texting have become our new norm of communication. Partners go to bed holding their computers instead of each other. This leaves us with little time to nurture each other and keep our happiness in perspective. All in all, this is a real set up for disconnection, disillusion and division.

Perhaps the divisiveness in our country is symbolic and a reflection of the divisiveness we face in our personal relationships—not just with our partners, but with family, friends and colleagues. We often find ourselves adding a new dimension to our relationships—wanting to be right instead of happy—and we soon find fault and the worst in each other rather than remembering what brought us together in the first place.

We seem to be living in surrealistic times, forced to face new norms. This may be the exact time when we need to slow down, shop less, work together, turn off our electronic devices, and heaven help us—even limit our television time!

It is important to develop a "team" effort to move forward to restore our relationships. Maybe we need to re-evaluate what is really important, to become aware of our strengths as well as our weaknesses, and to make the changes needed so that we can grow old together and build a healthier model of living for our children and grandchildren. Let's hope it's not too late.

The Legend of the Lost Libido
or a Primer on Sex Addiction
and Sexual Dysfunction

Most people think of sexual dysfunction in men as something related to erectile dysfunction (ED), whether it's pre-mature ejaculation, impotency, or an inability to ejaculate. In women, this takes the form of frigidity, an inability to climax or achieve orgasm or vaginal pain during stimulation or intercourse.

Hypoactive sexual desire disorder (HSDD), now known as female sexual interest/arousal disorder, is a sexual dysfunction that causes a lowered sex drive in women. Many will pass off the symptoms of HSDD as the inevitable effects of aging or changes in their body.

Both genders can exhibit a loss of libido. Physical issues that can cause low libido in men include low testosterone, prescription medicines, too little or too much exercise, and as stated before, alcohol and drug abuse and other assorted addictions.

We already know that psychological issues in men and women can include depression, anxiety, low self-esteem, stress, and unresolved problems in relationships. If these issues go untreated, they will eventually destroy what was once so special.

There is much more to sexual dysfunction than meets the eye. Although controversial, sexual dysfunction can also include sexual addiction, the opposite of all we have mentioned here.

Barbara's Story

The following story is an example of sexual dysfunction portrayed as a sex addiction, coupled with cross addictions, including drugs, alcohol, an eating disorder and compulsive shopping. This is Barbara's cautionary tale:

> I stood alone, not for the first time, with a sense of pride and humility, holding a microphone in my hands once again, about to share

my story. I looked around the room and saw the faces of so many brethren trying to pull their lives together, many called "the old timers," some called "newcomers," and then those who had relapsed and were trying sobriety a second, third or who knows how many times again. I was here in my meeting, what I had come to call my new home, and was celebrating my first year of abstinence. My hands were shaking and I thought my knees were going to buckle. A wave of heat ran through my body. I glanced across the room and focused on the one man who had helped make this day happen. His name was Al and he had been in AA for 35 years, and yet we were on the same journey. I knew that if he could do it, I could too. He looked at me as if there was no one else in the room and gave me a smile of confidence. It was as if he were saying what I was thinking, so I cleared my throat and began to speak.

"Oh boy! Where do I begin? I've had a great life, one that most women would envy. I had beauty, brains, and a loving husband who was a very successful lawyer. I lived in a gorgeous home on the water, with three beautiful kids, and time to do whatever I wanted, with no questions asked, and time to get into so much trouble. However, time, or too much of it, wasn't the culprit. It was my addictions. I was an alcoholic, cross-addicted with cocaine, shopping, and assorted sexual-enhancing drugs, and of course, men. I was an insatiable addict with an eating disorder to boot! I never did anything in a small way. I had a greedy appetite for everything. But my drug of choice was alcohol.

Although I stopped the use of all other drugs except alcohol, men were still up there in the running. Even while married, I had at least two boyfriends, sometimes at the same time, and each one never knew about the other.

The fact that I can share my story is a miracle. I should have been dead at least three times, and not from the drugs. My choices were crazy because I was rarely clean and sober. For most of adult life, in fact, my moods were artificially altered.

My childhood and teen years were filled with whatever I wanted, whenever I wanted and wherever I wanted. Most of those things should never have been allowed. However, my parents were addicts, my siblings were addicts and the only way they knew how to love us was to let us get away with whatever we did. I was coddled, spoiled and over-indulged. I grew up with the idea that I could continue employing this winning formula without too many obstacles, and I learned early on how to bamboozle everyone.

I didn't know or understand any of this when I married Carl. In fact I really didn't know much of anything, although I thought I was hot shit. I had a law degree and no idea what to do with it. I was uncertain about any of my future. I mean, who has any insight at 24?

Carl and I met in law school. I know that sounds amazing. I had the smarts and the tenacity to see it through. But it felt like an accident that I was even accepted. I was cocky, aggressive and arrogant, but that was just a cover up for my insecurities since my addictions had not yet fully blossomed.

Carl was three years ahead of me. I was just starting when he was finishing. He looked nothing like a lawyer, more like The Marlboro Man, but he never smoked cigarettes. He was a bit rough around the edges, with rugged features, the kind of guy who turned you on or not, nothing halfway. To me, his lack of good looks made him attractive. He was straight as an arrow, tough as nails (on the outside, that is), and sported a new Jaguar instead of a horse. Best of all, he didn't act like a lawyer. He was gentle and kind and had more integrity and humility than anyone I had ever known. Carl came from a very intellectual and severely dysfunctional family. Mine was just dysfunctional. His mom was a writer and his dad was a physician. My parents were well-heeled, but my dad was in business, (often the wrong kind) and my mother never worked outside the home. My dad was a high-functioning alcoholic and my mother was your classic co-dependent spouse. I got both—the alcohol addiction and the co-dependency.

I guess my saving grace was that even though our family was highly dysfunctional, there was plenty of love to go around. We were enmeshed, according to my therapist, but I always saw it as love.

At an early age, I took on the role of caretaker/rescuer. I was the youngest of five children, and in many ways filled the role of the eldest, even though I had been pampered and spoiled. I coached and nurtured my mother and siblings. Dad had his own agenda and was not interested in my opinion, or anyone else's, when it got right down to it. He had plenty for me, though. He told me how to dress, how to wear my make-up, my hair, etc. and some of his compliments felt laced with inappropriate language. I often felt exploited and "icky."

Carl and I were so happy. He joined a large law firm, well known in our community and nationally, too. He had a great opportunity to develop his area of interest in tax law. I graduated three years later, and we were married. Our life seemed magical, like a movie. I made him laugh and he made me feel special. I felt safe with Carl, as though nothing bad could ever happen. When I was in his arms, life was perfect. We spent most of our spare time in bed and soon out on the boat he bought for our first anniversary. I conceived about six weeks after we were married, so there went my career. In all honesty, it was never something I wanted to pursue. I wanted to be married and pregnant, and hoped to have lots of kids. When our first child was born, it seemed like life couldn't have been better.

All that changed as time passed and I grew deeper into my addictions. The nature of addictions are insidious so I wasn't aware of the hold they had on my body and spirit. It just seemed like part of my lifestyle. Carl also drank and did recreational drugs, but it was different for him. He was able to go to work and not use, except on weekends. It was not like that with me. I used continuously. I always seemed to have a glass of wine in my hand. I partied with friends, men and shamefully drank and used drugs during my pregnancies.

As time passed, I abandoned most of the drugs, except for the alcohol. My eating disorder went unnoticed until Carl caught me purging one morning. He said that he had been suspicious of an eating disorder for a long time because my behavior reminded him of when his sister was bulimic. He recognized the symptoms. After months of arguing and denying, I subjugated my will and went reluctantly into a 28-day treatment center for eating disorders. Although I learned a lot and attempted to participate in the work, part of me remained the addict who resisted treatment and refused to see her own addictive components.

I always believed I could stop the behavior whenever I chose. I was in denial. The treatment team tried to address my cross addictions, but like my parents and Carl, I manipulated them into thinking that I had it under control. Not that any of it was a waste of time. I learned a lot, but my other addictions took over my sense and sensibilities, so I managed to convince everyone that I was clean and ready to start my sober life. I had learned this well from my father and brothers so I was good at selling everyone, myself included, a bill of goods, and I did this way too often.

I became pregnant with my second child soon after I was discharged from the center and was able to stop drinking. The minute I was no longer pregnant, we both went to the bottle—baby and me! Carl noticed it, but I guess he didn't want to see the dangers it posed to our relationship and the kids. He would confront me, but I would have a tantrum or somehow convince him I was not out of control.

All my behaviors pointed to trouble.

My drinking kept me in an altered state. Men kept me juggling my life style, and both kept me from being the kind of wife and mother I wanted to be. Today, this remains my biggest regret.

I was not present for our children, yet I continued to have more. By the time our third child was conceived, I was well on my way to hell. I managed not to drink heavily during the pregnancy, but gulped a sip of wine whenever I could get away with it. Although it was something I knew was not right, I found ways to rationalize it and manage my addiction. It was like I was living two lives—one with Carl and the kids and one with my other lover and family, also known as my addictions.

Each time I went into treatment, which happened several times, I realized that I was never ready to be treated. I manipulated my way out of anything and everything, controlling everyone around me, until one day I could no longer manage my life. I had no more wiggle room. I guess that was when I hit bottom. They say that until that day happens, you really aren't ready for recovery.

Prior to that, I engaged in multiple affairs and crossed every boundary imaginable. I fucked my friend's husbands, my fitness instructor, who was also married, neighbors who showed me any attention and more men than I care to admit. Let's just say I had no will or simply one that ran riot. I don't know if the booze made my appetite for sexual conquests insatiable, or if my sexual encounters, which were many, made me drink more to drown my thoughts and rip out every shred of moral fiber I might have had.

I was drowning in my addictions. I lost complete sight of reality; not that I was psychotic, but I couldn't see the harm I was causing, not to my kids, Carl or myself. I was falling deeper and deeper into a hole that was tearing us apart and destroying our lives.

At that point, I was spiritually bankrupt. My choices with men were disastrous. They were sociopaths, losers or mentally unstable. I put myself in harm's way more than once, and each time when I was assaulted, I called Carl. He always came to my rescue, even long after we eventually separated. He tried to convince me to get my life together, but all the king's horses and all the king's men couldn't put this Humpty Dumpty back together again.

Sex with Carl became unbearable. I was insulting, critical and cruel. I made him feel less than a man. I told him he didn't know how to satisfy me, that he was a lousy lover and his cock was too small. The sad thing was, Carl and I were so well-suited for each other. We fit! At least in the beginning, we did. I changed all that. My drinking made me abusive and vitriolic, and I made him responsible for my feelings. Carl didn't stand a chance. He tried so hard to make it right, but no matter how hard he tried my drinking stood in our way. He didn't deserve my wrath and I placed him in a "no win" position.

Every time I share this, I cry.

I filed for divorce, probably because I sold myself another bill of goods, that Carl and I no longer work as a couple.

He was devastated, as everything about our family fell apart. I remained stubborn and drunk while Carl was confused and dismayed. He had no choice. I wanted out, but Carl had a trump card that I couldn't beat. He threatened to take the kids away and go for full custody if I continued to drink. The law would support that, and I knew it. That was the day I saw the light. That was the day I chose recovery.

It has been a long journey, one I will stay in for the rest of my life.

AA, my therapist and group, my sponsor and some of the members of the fellowship have all pulled me out of my hell hole. I have worked the program one day at a time and now, when I am celebrating my one-year birthday, I can't believe I have become so clear, so conscious and so grateful. I am still working on my moral inventory, making amends and dealing with all my regrets. The Twelve Steps have guided me through the eye of the needle. The steps have been my salvation. They have healed and liberated my wounded spirit. My fellowship has given me the courage and the support I so desperately need and my therapist has helped heal my wounded child and bring back my authentic self, which has been buried for so long under all my addictions.

I have my life back, but don't think for one moment that I don't know it can slip away from me if I don't stay diligent and dedicated to my recovery. One day at a time is my mantra.

The Serenity Prayer is my lifeline to reality.

I don't have a boyfriend now. I have learned that I need to have a relationship with myself before I can have one with another human being. That's why the program asks you not to get into a relationship for at least a year when you enter recovery. It takes that long to find yourself, and getting involved with another person will only prevent or delay that wonder from happening.

Carl and I are friends now. He is proud of my recovery and growth. We work together as parents in the best interests of our children. They are aware of my recovery. Our lives have become normal and healthy. We treat one another with respect, dignity and consideration.

I don't know what the future holds, but I know that whatever it will be, it will be better than anything I have experienced. Every day I wake up and thank God for making me an alcoholic. If not, I would not be the person I am today.

What Do We Do Now?

Barbara's story, while haunting and horrible, is also quite uplifting. She demonstrates that no matter how low any of us may go, we always have a chance for redemption. One thing that sticks out for me is how she found a support system and cultivated it in a way that slowly but surely has yielded positive, life-changing results.

Any of you currently struggling with sexual dysfunction and any related issues, take heed: if Barbara could turn her life around, so can you! Don't be afraid to seek the help you need, whether it's therapy, a change in diet or exercise or digging deep to find out what is really causing strife in your relationship or marriage. Above all, make sure you are being honest with yourself and communicating openly and effectively with the person you care about most.

We are only as sick as our secrets.

—**Alice Miller**, MD

10
Coping with Post Traumatic Breakup Disorder (PTBD)

I created the diagnostic term, Post Traumatic Breakup Disorder (PTBD), to call attention to the "condition" so many women face when their relationship or marriage comes to an end. You won't find this unconventional designation in the traditional Diagnostic, Statistical Manual for Mental Disorders DSM 5 because I made it up for the purpose of this chapter. It's doubtful to appear in the lexicon of classical psychiatry because even though it can cause Post-Traumatic Stress Disorder (PTSD) and even worse, homicide, and suicide, PTBD is not yet considered worthy of a place in the big book of disorders. For now, this affliction is known in the trade as PTSD or an adjustment disorder with mixed emotional features, such as depression and/or anxiety. In all honesty, though, no matter what you call this, it means you're fucked!

PTBD can happen from inside-out or outside-in. In the vernacular of psychology, an *endogenous* depression is usually a result of your genetic or biological constitution, which is most often predisposed from birth. It's the way your brain is wired. An *exogenous* depression is caused by external stimuli, which results in one form or another of a mood disorder, such as what we see in classical forms of depression and/or anxiety.

In the case of PTBD, it is definitely caused by something outside yourself—in this case, him! When a man declares an end to your relationship and you do not have any control over his decision, this will cause sleepless nights, bingeing or a loss of appetite, panic attacks, diarrhea, and occasionally, infantile rage. A traumatic break-up causes your neuro-generative functions to go awry. Seeing photos, hearing songs you shared, or passing streets you enjoyed walking along together can trigger all your visual, auditory and kinesthetic anchors. These unexpected moments produce tears, shortness of breath and deep sighs—signals that your heart is breaking. When this behavior leads to hours of conversations with whomever will listen to you dump your heartache on them, it can even make you vomit, like Jill Clayburgh did in the 1978 movie, *The Unmarried Woman*, when her husband announced, much to her chagrin, that he was in love with another woman and wanted a divorce. The awful shock of learning this threw Clayburgh's character into a panic and she quickly became unglued, or as we say off the record, she was fucked!

What Happens When a Relationship Breaks Up?

No matter how this goes down, it soon becomes a nightmare that feels like it will never end, especially when you didn't see it coming. What actually occurs when your investment of time, energy and emotions come tumbling down like Jack and Jill, destroying all your hopes, wishes and dreams? What are the physical and emotional ramifications of this disorder, which can leave you feeling so hopeless and desperate that just taking a shower seems too tough to handle? What goes on inside you when a break-up renders you totally dysfunctional?

PTBD can elicit a level of grief that carries a cascade of emotions, which feel interminable and take on a life of their own. Some manifestations of a broken heart can take weeks, months and even years to heal and overcome, especially if the essence of a relationship was built upon an addiction to love—a drug of choice for many women.

The physical and emotional symptoms, which accompany a broken heart can actually produce palpable pain in your chest and a feeling that part of you is sick and even disappearing. Heartache is real and a common effect of a break-up. You're not crazy! Sleepless nights, erratic weight gains or losses, a devalued sense of identity and a diminished sense of self-worth are all familiar signs of a broken relationship. If you are experiencing crying spells when you least expect them, sudden outbursts, stomach aches, headaches, diarrhea, murderous rage, frustration, and a feeling that this will never pass—you are having normal reactions to a breakup, especially when it was not your choice.

Losing faith and trust in the opposite sex often accompanies these symptoms. In *Something's Gotta Give*, Diane Keaton plays a prominent playwright who reluctantly collapses her rigid boundaries and falls in love with Jack Nicholson, a recording company mogul with a serious commitment phobia. Once he breaks through her defenses, which she had successfully maintained since her divorce, she loses control and surrenders her love-starved body, mind and soul to Nicholson, who is unable and unwilling to sustain a monogamous relationship. In an effort to discharge her pain and suffering, Keaton's character writes a play about her relationship, all the while crying her eyes out while pounding her fingers onto the keyboard. Writing her story was her unique way to heal her heartbreak. Any woman watching this movie could have had the identical emotional experience at some time in her life. Watching the film unfold, you don't know whether to laugh or cry, as you share these feelings of loss and grief. One thing is for certain, however. The older we get, and the more relationships we have, the better equipped we might become for dealing with the effects of when they don't work out as we hoped.

Dumpers and Dumpees

Whether you are the one initiating the break-up or you're on the receiving end of this tragic news, the feelings of the dumper are different than that of the dumpee. Both suffer, but with different emotions and subsequent experiences.

The dumper is usually relieved that the relationship is over, but he or she can experience a sense of guilt, self-doubt and shame. At the same time, the dumpee is devastated, confused, sad, often nauseous, grief-stricken and feeling lost, usually accompanied by a loss of interest in everything. Just getting by day to day requires an all-out effort. Feelings of abandonment, loneliness, apathy, self-degradation and even suicidal ideation are not uncommon.

Women who decide to end a relationship can experience the same emotions as a man. Even when they considered the relationship to be destructive to their well-being, and had solid evidence to support their decision, they can feel deep regret and self-doubt about their decision.

To be fair, men can also experience pain and suffering when they are dumped. The difference is, men traditionally compartmentalize better than women and take a more practical approach to handling rejection. They will feel the loss but they can overcompensate by acting out or diving into their work.

In *Something's Gotta Give*, Nicholson immediately continued his conquests with much younger women in an effort to avoid commitment and heartache. This may have temporarily masked his grief, but it couldn't erase the loss of being with the only women he may have ever really loved. His heartache morphed into a heart attack, which was soon determined to have been caused by stress, which we can easily recognize as unacknowledged grief.

You're Not Alone

PTBD is a universal human experience. Divorce statistics show that "for better or worse" is no longer a cultural expectation. We live in an age when people marry later and women are more independent and don't have the same needs as their mothers and grandmothers. Men are more dedicated to finding a successful career than a successful partner, even when their mothers may pressure them to marry and produce grandchildren. This is a generalization, however, in my practice it seems to be the norm.

I have also seen a consistent pattern when it comes to the important distinction between losing a relationship that was based on healthy, adult love and one that was based on some level of co-dependency. In those cases, the pain lasts longer than six months to a year, which often causes a clinical depression, requiring anti-depressant and/or anti-anxiety medication. When this occurs, it is often a sign of co-dependency or a love addiction. When a woman feels as if she can't go on without a man, that he, and only he makes her complete, and that her world and happiness depends on him, you can be sure that she had a co-dependent relationship. If her suffering lingers for more than a year then she is showing all the signs of a classic love addict!

If that is the case, someone needs help!

Get to a CODA or Love Addicts Anonymous meeting or find a therapist who specializes in co-dependency and love addiction. There is a reason why the struggle to let go is so interminable. It has to do with the history that is brought into the relationship, especially when a woman hopes it will make her past better in the present. Stop. That never works. Whether this is going on with a woman you know or it's you suffering through it, you are the only one who can heal the past in order to make better choices in the present.

But remember, PTBD is all too common and you are not alone.

"Did I Ever Really Matter?"

I hear this question over and over in my office. You probably did in the first stage of the relationship, but as time went on, his interest waned and he left you for his own reasons, some of which he may have shared, or perhaps not.

The usual answer, if you are lucky enough to receive one, usually goes like this:

"It's not about you. It's me. It's just not working for me."

When you want to learn more and understand his shift from "I love you" to "It's not working," you may just get a shrugging of his shoulders and an "I'm sorry," or even worse he may tell you that, "I met someone else."

That's the one that puts a fire in your belly and sends you into shock. This unexpected dismissal throws you into a den of destruction, with no way to find solace. You are bewildered, broken, beyond words that make any sense and left with feelings of betrayal and abandonment.

In other words, you're fucked and there is nothing you can do about it.

You find yourself listening to music with words that define your broken relationship and mental anguish. The lyrics and emotion of Mariah Carey's Can't Live if Living is Without You haunt you morning and night, filling your head with words that could have been written by you.

"No I can't forget tomorrow when I think about my sorrow....

I can't live if living is without you, I can't give anymore...."

You wake up each morning with those phrases filling your head with words describing exactly how you feel, wondering from the moment his words of good-bye sent you reeling into disbelief if you are still stuck in the nightmare of your relationship being over. Knowing that you can't do a damn thing about it creates a perpetual churning feeling in your stomach, filling up every cell of your body, and it never lets you forget that you've been fucked. Right now, it doesn't matter if you ever really mattered, because right now you just don't—not to him, at least, but here's the moment it can turn so that you do matter to yourself. One of my patients has lived through quite a story herself, and her experience offers us lessons.

Brenda's Brutal Break-up

Brenda called me four times, starting at nine in the morning until five in the afternoon. Her language was muffled with sobs and sighs so deep that I could hear her gasp repeatedly in between her almost inaudible messages.

"What's going on Brenda? You left four messages since this morning. You know I don't respond to phone calls until the end of the day."

"But it was urgent. I was having a meltdown."

"You know the drill. If you are having an emergency, you go to the hospital. That's what my voice mail explicitly says."

"Well, it wasn't a real emergency. I just didn't know what to do. I felt like I couldn't breathe. I began vomiting and couldn't even get a sip of water down."

"That's an emergency, Brenda. Why didn't you just go to the emergency room?"

"It would have been too embarrassing and I knew you would be the only one who could get me through it. Jacob left. He's gone, never coming back. Says he's had it. Done! Kaput! Oh my God, I hate him. I hate him!"

Her sobbing mixed with her hysterics.

"This is something that is not going to be fixed over the phone, Brenda. You need to come in and address this issue. A surgeon can't do surgery if you are not in the operating room. Your meltdown needs to be treated in a clinical setting and not over the telephone."

"Can I come first thing tomorrow morning? I need your help. I don't know if I can get through the night without your support."

It took a few minutes to calm Brenda down. She had the emotional resources to help herself through this event, but she didn't quite believe it. After reassuring her that she would live through this and setting a time that worked for both of us, she made a noble effort to relax and waited anxiously until the following day for her appointment.

When Brenda came into my office the next afternoon, she did not appear relaxed at all. On the contrary, she looked as if she had been through a war zone. She had neglected to shower, put on any make-up or comb her hair. Brenda was a train wreck. The best visual example I can give is Ellen Burstyn in the movie *Requiem for a Dream*, when all her hopes and wishes dissolved into the stuff of dreams. Brenda said she hadn't slept all night and had taken more than her prescribed dose of Clozapine, the anti-anxiety medication prescribed by her psychiatrist.

I had been seeing Brenda weekly for about three months, working on her tumultuous relationship, which was clearly a classic case of co-dependency, another way to say she had a love addition.

She and Jacob had met online and there was an immediate collision. When a relationship begins like that, with a collision, I believe it usually ends in one. Brenda broke every rule in the book of online dating by using sex as her weapon of attraction. Jacob was soaking up her seduction. During the first six weeks of courting, with the exception of meeting life's necessities, like food, water, sleep, bathing, nature's callings and in their case, work, Brenda and Jacob spent all of their time between the sheets in an effort to cement a co-dependent relationship. Neither one of them were conscious of their intentions, and Brenda was certainly not conscious of creating a dependent relationship with me, her therapist.

For Brenda, talk therapy would be like never flushing the toilet. She needed some experiential family of origin work. As you might imagine, that was not her choice, so at this juncture she was given a choice: either capitulate to my direction or find another therapist. I explained that her need to discuss her relationship with Jacob was not helpful to her goal. It only fueled the grieving and served no positive purpose. After three months of treatment, she didn't even have an outcome goal. There was nothing on her horizon. I had to lead her into creating a vision so she would know what it would look like, sound like, feel like and how it would impact her life if she reached it. That took nearly three months to identify. Brenda was so invested and caught up in the story that finding a solution was her last concern. It was time for me to step in.

"Your way isn't working Brenda, so we have to move onto my way. We need to move into your childhood wounds and talk about what happened to you that you would allow yourself to sell your soul to the devil. You have been on a roller coaster ride with this *Don Juan* since your time in bed morphed into reality. This is not a movie—its real life. People don't spend their nights fucking their brains out and thinking that it's love; at least not healthy, mature adults."

Brenda looked at me like a lost child. She was a very attractive woman in her mid-50s, and had been through several *Don Juans*—different content, but the same results. They all ended in a break-up decided upon and executed by *Don Juan*. She had worked as a para legal for the same law firm for nearly 25 years. She was competent, capable, and resourceful. When it came to relationships, however, she had failed miserably. It was as if her brain had a hole in the neo-cortex related to her cognition. She dove directly into the reptilian portion, without giving a thought to the consequences. (Remember, alligators eat their own for survival.)

Each man was a legend in her mind—a conquest. Her stories, albeit different in content, were identical in their structure. They would meet at a bar. She would wear her most seductive attire and the conquest commenced. She would stare him down until she caught his attention. He would respond with a flirtatious glance, a wink and a smile. She would pucker her lips and blow him a kiss. Her dragon breath reached clear across the bar and he would draw it into his own. That's when the fireworks began. One would think that after a few times playing this sport Brenda would have learned a lesson, or at least she would have asked herself why she kept repeating the same history.

"Why does this keep happening? Why me? I'm a good person. I'm intelligent, good-looking and even sexy at my age. These guys can't get enough of me in the beginning, and then it dwindles to a farewell, and they usually blame themselves. I hate that. I fall in love and then out of nowhere, I'm not loveable anymore. What did I have that I don't have now? I'm the same woman they met in the beginning. I didn't change. If anything, I got better."

Brenda's whining and lamentations had me slipping into a corner of my mind, remembering Eydie Gorme's musical rendition of What Did I Have That I Don't Have Now? I quickly returned my attention to Brenda, curled up in the corner of my couch with tears rolling down her cheeks.

"I think the time has come for you to explore the reasons for your behavior. You are the one who made these choices. If we look deeply, perhaps we can discover the why's you keep asking about. Brenda, tell me about your childhood. What was it like growing up with your parents?"

"We don't have to go there. What happened in the past is in the past. I had a good childhood. My father and mother worked hard to support us. They never made much money but they tried hard to please my brother and me. My father drank a bit, but he wasn't an alcoholic. My mother never seemed to be happy. I don't think I had ever seen a smile on her face or heard any laughter, but I know they loved us and did the best that they could, given their circumstances. I really don't want to go there. It brings up some bad memories that I don't want to think about. Can't you just tell me what I need to do to stop this crazy merry-go-round?"

"I just did. Wherever you don't want to go is exactly where you *need* to go."

Brenda looked disappointed.

"Look, my parents had their problems, but they did the best they could. I don't want to blame them for my problems. I made poor choices and now I am bearing the consequences."

"Yes, you are. You have paid your dues many times and here you are, at 55 years of age, and nothing has changed. Look, this isn't a blame game, Brenda. If we blamed your folks, we would have to go back and blame theirs, and theirs before them. That's not the way this works. Intentions don't matter in this work. You need to know what happened to you."

Brenda's eyes shifted towards the ceiling. She began to shake and tears rolled down her face as her sighs shifted to visceral sounds coming from her belly.

"What's going on? Let it come up! Bring it up, Brenda. Give it words—let it come up."

"I can't! I can't! Please don't make me!"

"Yes you can. You need to get it out—whatever it is. I'm here with you. I'm here for you."

No words came forth--just guttural, gut wrenching sounds mimicking a wounded animal. Brenda pulled her knees closer to her chest and buried her face into them.

"Brenda! Look at me now. Do you want to get well? Look at me—I'm right here."

After a few deep breaths, wiping her tears, she looked up with swollen, red eyes. Finally, she began to speak.

"My parents are Holocaust survivors. They were together at Auschwitz and were the only ones left from both their families. Nothing, nothing, nothing could be worse than what they suffered."

I waited for her sobbing to ease. It took only a few moments, but felt like hours. She looked at me like an innocent child, took a few more breaths and continued.

"I never wanted to go there. My heart hurts, just talking about it. My parents are wonderful people. They chose to be survivors, not victims. They struggled all their lives to take care of my brother and me, sacrificed everything so we would not feel deprived. They came to America through Israel. My brother and I were born there. I was three when we came to America. They worked long hours in a laundry, together, in the heat, with giant fans that never really cooled them down.

They each came home at night with damp clothes that had absorbed their sweat from the day.

My parents both came from a large family—seven siblings each, and they were the eldest. It was in those camps, those horrible camps, where both of their families perished. They were the only survivors. They never talked about it. My mother was 19 and my father 23. They were the lucky ones—or maybe they weren't. That's where they met, fell in love and survived."

I had no words in that moment that I felt would have sufficed, so I simply stayed present with my eyes, and waited.

"I'm so sorry Brenda. I didn't know. Three months together, and this is something I never knew. Thank you for sharing this. I know how difficult it must have been."

We both stayed silent together. Words were not needed. Brenda heaved a few more sighs, which were joined by mine.

"Enough, for now. There will be plenty of time for more. Let's just rest now. There's always another day."

I felt my own tears trying to find a way out. We sat for a few more minutes and I asked if I could share a meditation with her. Brenda nodded and allowed her body to relax into the sofa. We began with breathing.

"Close your eyes, Brenda. Be mindful of your breathing. It's the most fundamental rhythm of life—holding on and letting go. For now, you can hold on to as much as you like and you can let go to as much as you feel safe to do. Just be mindful of your breathing. The air that you breathe in and the air you breathe out...."

When Brenda returned the following week for her appointment she appeared more relaxed and volunteered that her mood had shifted since our last meeting.

"I reflected on our session all week," she said, "and realized that I had been holding in what I could not bear to express."

"Yes, I know. You've had this stored with lock and key in the basement of your mind and it was pleading to be released. Trauma gets locked in the amygdala part of the brain."

It was time to teach a little. I pointed to a large chart identifying the different parts of the brain. I began with the oldest part, the reptilian, and slowly identified each part.

"The reptilian is the oldest and most primitive part of our brain development asks the question, 'Am I safe and will I survive?' It's our fight or flight mechanism. It doesn't stop to think about consequences. It just does whatever it has to do in order to survive. The limbic system is the seat of our emotions and asks the questions, 'Is it painful or pleasurable?' Human beings run from pain toward pleasure. The neo-cortex is the computer in your brain and asks the question, 'Is it reasonable and logical? The reptilian could care less about reason and logic, as it only wants to survive. The limbic goes for pleasure to avoid pain. That's where the trauma is sealed—in the amygdala. It also doesn't care about outcomes or consequences. The neo-cortex, the limbic system and the reptilian brain do not interact with one another—unless we make that choice. They are independent and exist for their own agenda. It's up to the frontal lobe, the newest and most evolved part of our brain, to consider consequences and outcomes. It thinks about what the neo-cortex is thinking about. In other words, it is the mindful and conscious part of our brain. The intention is different in each part, with the exception of the neo-cortex and the frontal lobe. The others are there to protect you from feeling the pain, not unlike shock absorbers on a car."

I walked over to the chart I had read hundreds of times and used as a closing mantra in my groups. It was the one in the Gospel of Thomas that said, "If you bring forth what is within you, what you bring forth will save you. If you do not bring forth what is within you, what you do not bring forth will destroy you."

I read aloud it a few times and asked Brenda to read it, too.

"Read it with the intention of understanding the meaning as it relates to you."

Brenda repeated the words three or four times. She looked at me with a sense of curiosity and wonder.

"I get it. I get it. This is what I came here for."

I nodded, and smiled.

"How do the words resonate with you?"

"I understand. I have kept this as much as a secret as my parents. It always felt like an unspoken covenant. We knew it was there, but we were not comfortable asking questions. This is why I'm here."

"Yes, this is why you are here and why there was a shift from anxiety and enormous pain to understanding and serenity. You expressed what had been inside you for most of your life and you have been saved by your self-exploration, which has challenged your fears and all that has gone unspoken for so long. Maybe the most significant thing for you is, you had someone here to serve as a benign witness to your suffering and emotional exorcism. You are a courageous woman, Brenda—a real warrior."

She sat quietly for a long time, without saying a word, glancing back and forth at the charts I had just used to explain the brain and reading the quote from the gospel of Thomas.

"I get it. I get it. I was so unaware of what was behind my compulsion that I sacrificed myself in an effort to feel worthwhile and loved."

"Tell me more."

I leaned forward into her space to look at her with soft eyes.

"I think I took on my parent's feelings. Feelings that they didn't matter. Feelings of low self-worth and whatever leftovers they carried out of Auschwitz, which they never shared with my brother and me. I knew about the Holocaust and their time in the concentration camp, but they never talked about it. Whenever we would ask, they would say it was not something we should ever know. They were family secrets, but we knew, we always knew the horrors of their lives. I learned about it in high school with all the books I read and the movies I saw. I guess I tried to carry their feelings with me so they wouldn't have to carry them. I think my brother did the same. We both have never been able to find happiness and longevity in a relationship. We were carrying our parent's history, along with our own."

"Yes, Brenda, and perhaps now is the time to let it go. This history is not yours. You have unconsciously inherited your parents' trauma. Do not claim what is not yours. They would not want you to take on their legacy of the Holocaust. It would prolong the suffering to another generation. One was quite enough."

I felt Brenda finally letting go of much of the weight she had been carrying around for most of her life. Maybe she could finally allow herself to value her own existence.

What Do We Do Now?

What does Brenda's story mean for having a conscious relationship? It is important to know that being "woke" in a conscious relationship doesn't just apply to relationships with others, although it is essential for success. It also means connecting with your internal essence by getting in touch with your feelings, recognizing them as your own, and cultivating a conscious relationship with yourself. This requires asking fundamental questions, such as the following:

Who am I?

What is my purpose?

How do I want to live my life?

Who have I hurt?

What amends do I need to make?

How can I do the right thing?

These are the same questions, which Jews ask themselves on Rosh Hashanah, the Jewish New Year, and which curious people all over the world, no matter what their religion or culture might be, are also asking in one way or another. Even as things change over time, these philosophical questions remain as foundational components in the world of psychology and within cultures throughout the world. They reach beyond any religious doctrine, and we will address them in the next chapter.

If we can develop higher consciousness and mindfulness, especially in the context of our relationships, our lives will be enriched. If we can address each other with appreciative inquiry and respect, our relationships will thrive.

"Am I willing to make this commitment in order to have a fulfilling and meaningful life and a healthy and happy relationship?"

This is a question each of us must ask, and if you answer yes, then read on.

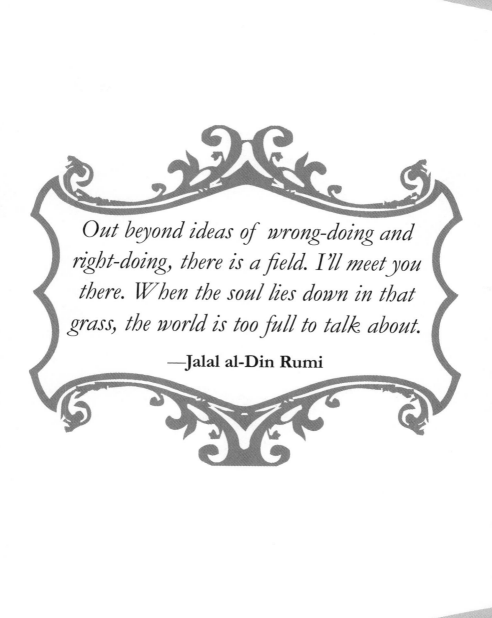

Out beyond ideas of wrong-doing and right-doing, there is a field. I'll meet you there. When the soul lies down in that grass, the world is too full to talk about.

—Jalal al-Din Rumi

11
A Conscious Relationship

After returning home from an Encounter-Centered Couples Therapy (ECCT) Master Class reunion in Ischia, Italy in May 2018, I received a letter from a woman named Judith, a colleague who helped coordinate the event and was reaching out to all of us who had attended.

Two months later, Judith passed away after a courageous, two-plus-year struggle with pancreatic cancer. She left a legacy of the lessons she learned during her fight, which complemented all of what she had practiced during her life's work. Her missive, which a portion of is included here, highlighted the most salient questions she had been asking herself just before she passed, even when she did not know her days were numbered.

A Love Letter

"When I let go of what I am, I become what I might be." ~ Lao Tzu

Hi dearest friends,

Saying good-bye has been difficult and coming back to Paris even more difficult. I guess you could say that I am experiencing 'separation anxiety'. I miss you all. Today I have felt lost, sad, tired, not wanting to eat and have been listening to music and hanging out in bed.

I have been reflecting on what is going on. I have been pondering this question all day. What has suddenly emerged is my experience during our gathering of love and secure attachment. Many of us have not known 'secure attachment' as a child. I, for one, did not and I have been working on this throughout my cancer journey with 'cellular memory' as an amazing tool.

I started thinking about the questions:

What is love, and what does it feel like to be 'securely attached'?

I am referring to love and secure attachment on an 'essence or soul level' rather than on an 'ego level'. The words I came up with were:

feeling loved for who I am, not what I do,

feeling safe,

feeling secure and that someone will protect me,

feeling seen,

feeling heard,

feeling able to be vulnerable,

feeling loving eyes,

feeling loving touch,

feeling cherished, adored, unique, special,

feeling appreciated for my differences and talents,

feeling accepted when my behavior is different than others.

The experience of this allows me to feel securely attached. The three days we spent together demonstrated all that for me. As each day went by, our connection deepened until there was a space of love and trust where I felt secure and safe and able to share with you deeply and honestly and to receive you with respect, love and curiosity.

Thank you, each and every one of you, for being who you are.

It was more than a three-day gathering of ECCT therapists for me. It was an experience about being with loving, accepting, highly conscious people who are able to make space to receive the other, fully and unconditionally. I feel that this experience will live on in me and my life will be different because of it.

I bow to each of you. I love you.

Judith

What Is a Conscious Relationship?

Judith was my beloved friend and kindred spirit, a wizard therapist, whose memory will live on within every soul she touched and every life she transformed. This book is dedicated to her.

Her responses are the best description I can offer to a question many of us should be asking: "What is a conscious relationship?" The answer doesn't suddenly emerge out of the blue. It is not acquired in a moment, a year or even for many, in a lifetime. It takes a genuine commitment to create and maintain conscious relationships as individuals and as couples. We are not born knowing how to do that, and developing the necessary skills, tools, resources and mindfulness takes practice and desire. While some may have parents who modeled a conscious relationship for us, this does not occur as often as we would like because every family is dysfunctional to some degree.

The term, "conscious relationship" didn't exist in most of our families of origin. Virginia Satir, the founder of family therapy and a wizard therapist in her own right, was considered a pioneer in the field of marriage and family therapy. She treated her first family in 1951, when doing so was considered an unconventional practice. We've certainly come a long way since then. It is only recently, in fact, perhaps in the last 30 years, that we have been able to discover the invaluable insights that therapists like Satir promoted, as we finally come to understand the importance of creating and maintaining conscious, mature, and healthy relationships.

Judith's whole life and career were dedicated to asking the right questions and recognize the appropriate answers. It was as if her understanding arrived just in time—two months before her demise, when she shared her introspective insights with us. Her generosity of spirit serves as an example of someone who kept searching for answers to questions, which most of us never even ask.

The tragedy of tragedies is to face your death and not know who you are. Judith searched deeply, inspired by Gerard Manley Hopkins, an English poet and Jesuit priest in the 1800s, who left us all a provocative quote: "What I am is me, for that I came." Judith's quest reminds me of Herman Hesse's *Siddhartha*, whose spiritual journey was one of self-discovery. In her own way, Judith exemplified and embraced the most important questions and answers we must learn and integrate on our own path to having conscious relationships. She and her beloved husband modeled the essence of this type of ultimate union.

A Litmus Test

Some of Judith's last words bear repeating:

> Many of us have not known 'secure attachment' as a child. I, for one, did not and I have been working on this throughout my cancer journey with 'cellular memory' as an amazing tool. I started thinking about the questions: What is love, and what does it feel like to be 'securely attached'? I am referring to love and secure attachment on an 'essence or soul level' rather than on an 'ego level'.

How do you relate to the feelings Judith described in her missive?
Are you loved for who you are and not what you do?
Do you feel safe?
Do you feel secure that someone will protect you?
Do you feel seen or heard?
Are you able to be vulnerable in your relationship?
Do you feel loving eyes, a loving touch upon you?
Do you feel cherished, adored, unique and special?
Do you feel appreciated for your differences and talents?
Do you feel accepted when your behavior is different than others?
If you have answered "yes" to these questions, then we can say that you are living and feeling securely attached in a conscious relationship.

If you have answered "no" too many times then it's time to learn how to achieve these essential feelings and to be able to learn how to share them equally with your partner. After all, you cannot give what you do not have.

Love, and Lessons from Oz

Love is difficult to define because it is subjective and means different things to different people. In his book, *The Road Less Traveled*, M. Scott Peck wrote what is one of the most brilliant definitions of love I have ever read:

"Love is the willingness to extend yourself in order to nurture another person's spiritual growth as well as your own."

Are you doing this in your relationship? If not, why not?

Here is your moment to explore these questions. Be brutally honest and accurate with your answers, as you must be true to yourself. It's easy to justify, defend, deny, project, blame and sell yourself a bill of goods. However, if you want to grow you must look inside. Once you do, you will begin practicing mindfulness and the art of consciousness.

Most people can't do this alone. They need a benign witness, a therapist trained to help navigate the process. It is not the wizard in *The Wizard of Oz* who leads Dorothy and her friends down the yellow brick road. She must wind her way through the dark green forest to find her way back home. The lion represents the courage she is seeking. The scarecrow symbolizes her mind, and the tin man, her heart. It is only when Toto, Dorothy's dog and security blanket, leaps out of her arms that her vulnerability transforms into empowerment. She is left alone to delegate and fight her way to freedom. When she does, she arrives at a place of true self-love.

The dark green forest filled with lions and tigers is there to motivate us, not deter us from finding ourselves. It's only after Dorothy kills the Wicked Witch of the West that her higher power appears in the form of Glenda, the Witch of the East. She comes down from the clouds and tells Dorothy to click her heels so she can return home to Kansas. Dorothy, distressed and weary from her search, yells back at Glenda.

"Well, why you didn't tell me that in the first place?"

"If I had, you wouldn't have believed me. You had to go through the dark green forest to find your way home."

This is exactly what needs to happen if we want to know ourselves. Not unlike Dorothy, or Judith, a seeker of truth, it takes time, patience and commitment to follow the yellow brick road and discover who we are. I am not sure if L. Frank Baum, the author of *The Wizard of Oz*, had any idea of the impact and meaning his story would have on self-discovery, but we can all be thankful he inspired the great artists of Hollywood to animate his splendid tale.

It's easier today to travel down the yellow brick road than it was for Dorothy and even Siddhartha. We have more practical ways to make the journey to self-discovery. Group therapy, a process I facilitated for 37 years, is perhaps the most successful modality I know of to learn about your essence. The feedback received from others, if taken into consideration with positive intention, can be so helpful, even to the most resistant and skeptical patient.

That's because there is always a window, which does not allow us to see what others find so easy to see in us. When the same issues keep rising up over and over, then you know these are patterns just begging to be addressed. So when a handful of fellow citizens give you the same feedback, only a fool would not consider listening and looking inside. The answers are there. It takes a conscious mind to allow the unconscious to emerge.

What is Mindfulness?

According to Mission Be, an organization devoted to promoting social learning and stress-reduction in schools, "Mindfulness can be described as the practice of paying attention in the present moment, and doing it intentionally and with non-judgment. Mindfulness meditation practices refer to the deliberate acts of regulating attention through the observation of thoughts, emotions and body states."

In today's whirling world of technology, hectic schedules, perennial responsibilities, obligations, life stressors and more, it is difficult to stay present and in the moment. It is an art to learn, not unlike presencing. That is why there are so many classes and programs today teaching mindfulness. Our world is spinning so fast that if we are not living in the moment and being mindful, it is easy to forget what really matters.

We need to take stock of what is truly important and what is not. What is important to a 30-year old is not as important as when you are

50 or 60 years old. When you reach my age of 80, it's all relative. Ask a 25-year-old what's important. You might get an answer of finding a soul mate, reaching career goals, staying fit and thin, having a nose job, a boob job, a bubble butt and so on. As we age, our interests and goals change. Staying healthy is vital. For a millennial, still young and taking life for granted, staying healthy is not as important as finding their passion, a boyfriend or girlfriend, spending three days at a music festival or passing the M-cats. Of course our culture has changed and young people are more aware than their parents ever were about the benefits of living a healthy lifestyle. They are also into mindfulness in ways that previous generations were not.

Looking ahead, I want them to know that growing old is not easy without a partner. If you are divorced, never married or widowed, it gets tougher. That's compounded if you are over the age of 60, because after living life alone, compromise can be difficult. One gets used to not having to make a bed, going to sleep whenever it's convenient, skipping a shower, eating eggs with ketchup, watching favorite TV shows with no compromise, and not having to deal with toilet seats that never get put down.

However, this solitary life can also be lonely and even depressing.

Are dating sites the answer? Creating a profile online can be risky, like walking through a minefield. Do you advocate for gun control? Are you a Trump supporter? Conservative or liberal? Any answer can trigger a deluge of negative responses or incite a small riot. You might find who you think is the perfect guy, but after a few dates and developing feelings for him, you learn that he is a recruiter for the NRA, which goes against your values as a gun control advocate. These issues never rose up a few years ago. You could have political preferences and differences, which may not be aligned, but now, almost any contrast can be a deal breaker. What's a girl to do? Be true to yourself. Be mindful before acting on a whim or through magical thinking. Remember what Freud said, which Deepak Chopra added to when he said, "There are no accidents! There is only some purpose that we haven't yet understood."

Differences will arise and cause conflict. It's easy to enter, but difficult to escape.

Re-learning the Golden Rule

What's all of this have to do with a conscious relationship? Everything! Consciousness and mindfulness are essential practices for having a quality relationship with yourself and your partner. The quote, "Physician, heal thyself," is applicable to knowing yourself—to attend to one's own faults, as opposed to pointing out the faults of others. Until you have a positive relationship with yourself, you will not be able to have a successful relationship with another.

It's never too late. In ECCT, couples counseling includes learning about yourself as well as your partner. It's not essential to go to individual counseling. Exploring your shortcomings, inhibitions, fears, and maladaptive behaviors can be successfully accomplished in the context of couple's therapy. ECCT provides the principles and rituals that create outcomes you might have never thought possible. It is truly what Schleifer espouses—"an adventure in intimacy."

This process is no different than the personal introspection Jews are asked to conduct on the High Holidays or addicts do as the 4th and 5th step of a 12-step program. It's all about delving deep into our souls, taking a moral inventory of our past, and making amends to those we have hurt while active in our addictions.

A moral inventory does not only include regrets and shameful behavior. It also includes recognizing the best of ourselves. The content may differ, but the structure of purging our souls from behavior that has hurt others is equal to the redemption we can find in making amends. In order to move forward, we must complete the past.

In the movie, *Flatliners*, medical students want to know what happens when we die. Each student take turns to see what they experience. As they are moved to the brink of death, they are brought back to life by the others, only to hear the same story repeated about making amends to those they hurt during their lifetime. None of them could go forth without doing so. We know this to be true in the concept of karma. In Hinduism and Buddhism, the sum of a person's actions in this and any previous state of existence is viewed as deciding their fate in a future existence. In real time, this means you must own your shadow side, review any of your past, which has caused pain and suffering to others, and make your amends. Apologizing to those who have been victims of your bad behavior must be owned as you ask for forgiveness.

The Bible supports the idea that you reap what you sow. In Job 4:8, it says that those who seek trouble usually find it. In Matthew 26:52, it indicates that those who are violent could come to a violent end. In Luke 6:37-38, it says, "Judge not, and you will not be judged; condemn not, and you will not be condemned; forgive, and you will be forgiven; give, and it will be given to you." These passages offer directions to us for how to live, with different resources pointing the way forward with the same intentionality.

On the first or second evening of a Tony Robbins workshop, he asks his participants to identify those who hurt them most in their lives and have caused unresolved anger and resentment. As a homework assignment, he requests that people go to their rooms and call perpetrators from their past who still have power over them because they are holding on to these negative feelings. He asks that they forgive them for their wrongdoings. This is not done for the benefit of the perpetrator. It is to free up energy, which is keeping those wounded souls stuck in the muck and mire of negative feelings, which are still there long after the original abuse.

This is an exercise in letting go. Anger and resentment are known as E-motions—energy in motion. While embodied in our minds and hearts, we absorb useless energy, which can be sublimated in productive and meaningful ways. By forgiving, you are actually liberating yourself and clearing the space for positive energy to enter. Forgiveness and making amends morph into happiness. Ponder that! Hard to believe we actually learned this basic stuff in kindergarten.

"Do unto others as you would have others do unto you!"

How quickly we forget.

What Do We Do Now?

It's time to step into the glorious abyss. Who have you hurt? Who has hurt you? What must you do to clean the slate? What is your take-away from reading this book? What questions remain unanswered? What do you need to do to assure that you can have a conscious relationship?

The answers are clear. Look deep and hard because if you are genuine and sincere in your search the answers lie within you. Why not reach out to those who can support your journey? Going into the unknown is always scary, but it's a vital part of the human experience. No one escapes. It's how we handle it. Do we have faith? Can we trust ourselves?

In her book *Feel the Fear and Do It Anyway*, Susan Jeffers offers insights and tools to deal with these existential issues. Nike says, "Just do it!" The subliminal message here might be, that if you can't do it alone, seek professional help. When Victor Frankl was asked how he coped with his experience in the concentration camps, he said faith and purpose was his answer, not hope. Hope comes and goes. Faith is forever. Purpose gives you the will to live.

"What was really needed was a fundamental change in our attitude toward life," Frankl said. "We had to learn ourselves and, furthermore, we had to teach the despairing men, that it did not really matter what we expected from life, but rather what life expected from us. We needed to stop asking about the meaning of life, and instead think of ourselves as those who were being questioned by life—daily and hourly."

We hear words of wisdom all the time. Many of them leave our conscious awareness moments after we hear or read them. Sometimes, these pearls appear as platitudes or clichés, because they are expressed so often, which can dilute their profound meaning. However, if you allow these messages to register, they can be valuable. Just sift through Facebook and Instagram and you will see them on a daily basis, making screensavers and soundscapes across our screens. I have many of them framed and hanging on the walls of my office. Sadly, I doubt that many take the time to read them. As you depart from my office, the first one, by a humble man called Abraham Lincoln, smacks you in the face.

"And in the end, it's not the years in your life that count. It's the life in your years."

Although words matter, they alone cannot effect change. Words do not have the power to transform our behavior or beliefs. Change comes from digging deep into the places we want most to avoid. It needs more than words of wisdom. If words were the answer, then all we would need to do is listen to the messages of Joel Osteen, Wayne Dwyer, Martin Luther King, Jr., Jesus, Moses, and all the prophets and sages who have graced the earth.

But the truth is, there is no magic fix for an internal problem with an external resolution. Whatever you do, don't keep doing the same thing over and over, expecting a different result.

Einstein said, "*You can never solve* a problem on the level on which *it* was created."

Do you really want to argue with Einstein? If you want an easy fix, watch Bob Newhart's *STOP IT!* on YouTube. If nothing else, you will get a good laugh. Meanwhile, take a chance on yourself, before after all, you're all you've got and that's plenty good enough!

Acknowledgments

This book represents the culmination of all the knowledge I have acquired over my 41-year career as a psychotherapist. It would be selfish of me not to share this with you, with the hope that you will benefit from my life's work. But this would not have been accomplished without the support of many people, and I want to acknowledge those who have made this possible.

First, my gratitude to all my clients who have defined so much of my professional life. Sharing in the time and effort it has taken to achieve their outcome goals has been enormously rewarding.

My deepest appreciation to Nancy Rosenfeld, my literary agent, who always believed in this book and encouraged me to have it published.

I want to extend my gratitude to my editor, David Tabatsky, whose talent took a diamond in the rough and polished and cut it into a gem, and to Hedy Schleifer, whose wisdom and teachings lent substance and knowledge to its content.

My deepest appreciation to Don Lessne, who by some divine intervention, learned about the book and thought it worthy of being published by his company, Frederick Fell Publishers Inc.

I feel honored and blessed that you, my readers, bought this book and helped to make it known to others. You are all part of the fabric that will hopefully make this a best seller!

Lastly, I want to thank my children, Monica, Todd, Erika, and Aaron, and my fur baby, Minnie, for their patience and understanding as I took the time and energy to write it.

Love,
Joan

About the Author

Joan E. Childs, LCSW, has been in clinical private practice as a psychotherapist since 1978. A clinical social worker, Joan specializes in couple's therapy, known as Encounter-Centered Couples Therapy. In addition, she is an expert in Co-dependency, Inner-child Work, Original Pain Work and Second Stage Recovery. She was the first affiliate of the John Bradshaw Center in the United States. She is a certified Master Practitioner for Neuro-linguistic Programming, a certified EMDR Master Practitioner, a certified grief counselor, a certified hypnotherapist, and PAIRS LEADER (Practical Application for Intimate Relationship Skills). Childs provides a two to five day intensive for individuals and a two-day intensive for couples in crisis. She has appeared on many national television shows, including *The Oprah Winfrey Show*.

Joan is the author of *The Myth of the Maiden: On Being a Woman* (HC Books 1995) and *Why Did She Jump? My Daughter's Battle With Bipolar Disorder* (HCI 2014), which is currently in pre-production for a film. She had her own television series, SOLUTIONS, dedicated to the memory of her daughter, Pamela Ann Glassman, which provided information and resources for the community, especially for patients and families with loved ones suffering from mental and mood disorders. She is the founder of the Pamela Anne Glassman Educational Center, in cooperation with the Mental Health Center of South Florida.

Joan's fourth book, *Staying Sane and Single*, is currently being represented by Nancy Rosenfeld, from AAA Books Limited, Inc.

Joan has published many articles on women's issues, relationships, grief and loss, which have appeared in several well-known online publications, including The *Huffington Post*.

To learn more about Joan, please visit her website,
www.joanechilds.com.

Index